THE SECRETS OF

EFFECTIVE

COMMUNICATION:

*HOW TO MAKE YOUR CONVERSATIONS
MORE MEANINGFUL, SPEAK
CONFIDENTLY AND STAY IN CONTROL AT
WORK, HOME AND IN RELATIONSHIP*

Diego De Giovanni

Table of Contents

Book Description

Do you want to change your life by improving your communication?

Are you ready to learn the art of communication?

Do you want to build trust and strengthen your relationship with effective communication?

Do you want to learn how to communicate effectively with coworkers, friends, kids and your partner?

In this book, we'll be taking a look at some of the most significant elements of change that you can introduce to your life if you want to communicate effectively. Everything written in this book is designed with the idea of helping improve your life and make you an effective communicator.

This book will provide you a set of proven techniques which can help you to transform your life by improving your day to day communication. You'll discover:

- Elements of effective communication

- The importance of body language in communication

- How to communicate with strangers?

- How to build friendship?

- Importance of effective communication

- How to make others feel special through communication?

By using this book and the information inside, you can begin the process of positively transforming Does this sound like the kind of treatment that you want to put in place? Then this book will help you do just that.

In this book, you'll find easy step-by-step instructions on how to communicate effectively under the following headings:

- THE ART OF EFFECTIVE COMMUNICATION

- ELEMENTS OF EFFECTIVE COMMUNICATION

- PRINCIPLES OF EFFECTIVE COMMUNICATION

- APPLYING COMMUNICATION SKILLS WHEN COMMUNICATING WITH STRANGERS

- HOW TO COMMUNICATE WITH PEOPLE TO BUILD FRIENDSHIPS

- MAKE YOUR CONVERSATIONS UNIQUE AND MEMORABLE

- COMMUNICATING WITH DIFFICULT PEOPLE

- USE LAUGHTER TO LIGHTEN THE CONVERSATION

Turn the page of your old life by Buying this book now. Make a step to your new, better future.

Introduction

The art of communication is essential to have for anyone to succeed in any field. People use their communication skills to convey their thoughts, feelings and emotions to others. Although all of us communicate in our own way but very few of us know how to communicate effectively.

Learning to effectively communicate takes time and practice, but it can easily be done with enough devotion to your new skill.

Effective communication determines your career success, your relationships with your spouse and other family members, your feeling of being appreciated and understood.

If you want to know how to acquire these skills and become a real master of speech, read on.

Chapter 1: The Art of Effective Communication

Good communication is the difference between a good and poor leader, a thriving and a boring relationship and an effective professional and an indifferent one.

Since you are living at a time when communication has never been better, all the more that you need to keep up with the changes and the means by constantly and diligently working on your communication skills. As a start, you can keep reading to better understand what and how communication works.

Communication is the act or process of conveying information, thoughts and ideas from one person to another in the form of speech, written words, signals, body language, visuals or behavior.

Great conversations almost always start with small talk. Many people avoid small talk at all cost. Sure, it can sound rather pointless to go on and on about the weather or the traffic. But such small talk serves as a precursor for breaking the ice and paving the way for truly significant conversations.

Maintain an active presence with your body language. Avoid fidgeting or looking over your shoulder like you're already mapping your way out. There should also be no scrolling on your phone. This can come across as plain disrespectful. Maintain comfortable eye contact. Such a posture will keep the conversation going.

What if you initiate small talk and the listener seems blank? Perhaps you're dealing with a conversation rookie who is still getting over social anxiety. Here, you have to speak some more of yourself to prod a response. Let's say you've met in a work seminar and you ask, 'Is this your first time here?' The person answers with a 'no', then awkward silence. You can add something more about yourself. 'Oh, I've been here before, although the speakers are different this year.' The person is then likely to ask about the previous year's speakers. There! You have a conversation going.

When communicating with others, there are three primary steps that occur - thought, encoding and decoding. If you're the sender, it starts from the information that resides in your mind or otherwise known as thoughts. Encoding happens if you decide to send the message to another person through words or other forms. Finally, decoding completes the process as the receiver translates the thoughts into something he or she understands.

Content is one and it refers to the actual words used when sending the message which is also known as language. The second element is context which refers to the way you delivered the message or otherwise referred as paralanguage. This element encompasses other key communication elements such as body language, gestures, eye expression, emotion and tone of voice.

Unfortunately, even though you've been communicating all your life, misunderstanding words and messages is a common occurrence of everyday life. Every person has different ways of interpreting words and context. You may think that you've communicated your ideas clearly but the receiver may not really fully grasp the importance or the full meaning of the message due to numerous communication barriers.

Anything that prevents you from conveying the message clearly and from the receiver understanding it correctly is considered a communication barrier. Barriers can be psychological or physical and the most common you'll probably face often include differences in culture, background, perception, bias, environment, noise and stress. In some instances, the message itself can be a barrier too especially if the focus is on the facts rather than the idea or message being transmitted.

Since most barriers are external and inherent to the receiver, communicating effectively is a tough feat to take on. Even so, it is one endeavor worth your effort. The key is to focus not on yourself but on the person or people you are trying to communicate to. Forget about being defensive, your ego or the need to feel superior if you truly want to be an effective communicator. Only by aspiring and training yourself to overcome communication barriers will you truly unleash the power of effective communication to every aspect of your life.

Chapter 2: Elements of Effective Communication

In a world where communication is a vital part of living and interacting, it is imperative to develop the right skills to make the process as effective as possible. If you want to get ahead at work, connect more with people and be a better leader, having good communication skills is your gateway to success.

Whether you're the sender or receiver of the message, there are important factors you need to constantly work on in order to master the art of communicating effectively.

Speech

One of the most obvious forms of communication is speech. This is basically the verbal aspect of the process where words are used to convey the message. When speaking, it is important to keep it short and simple. That is, focus on the important matters and use the right words to deliver your thought as plainly as you can.

Words that come from your mouth may be only 10% of communication but it is just as equally important as other elements. To truly learn the skill, you need to master how to use the right words when interacting with a diverse group of people.

Body Language

This nonverbal form of communication covers body movement, hand gestures, facial expressions, eye contact and posture. These are nonverbal cues that you need to use and take note of if you want to communicate effectively.

When listening to someone talk, pay attention to body language for better insight about the other person's feelings and attitude. You should make eye contact whenever possible or you may nod occasionally to convey agreement. You should also maintain excellent posture and never cross your arms. In other words, match your body's language with your words to avoid confusion on the part of the receiver.

Tone of Voice

Knowing the correct tone to use is critical for effective communication because the right tone can convey the right emotion. Whether you want to be authoritative, friendly, passive or convincing, it's all a matter of injecting the correct tone that will help influence the other person and understand your underlying message more accurately.

Active Listening

Another essential skill you need to master is active listening. When communicating with other people, you're not only a talker but you should also be a good listener. And it's not just about hearing words, filtering it and choosing only what you want to understand.

Active listening is paying attention not just to the words but also to body language and tone.

Also part of active listening is to avoid interruption when the other person is still talking. Wait for your turn and while doing so stay focused on the conversation at hand. Avoid articulating your responses in your mind and more importantly, avoid making judgments. Whether you agree with the person you are communicating with or not, judgment should be reserved and set aside.

Stress Management

With stress in the picture, you or the person you are talking to will see things differently. The way you think, act and respond may be disrupted leading to confusion and misunderstanding. To avoid sending out mixed nonverbal cues and unhealthy negative behaviors, you need to know how to manage stress. For some people, meditating helps while others exercise or go for a run to temper the problem.

There is no one standard formula to managing stress. They key is to find out ways that work for you.

Chapter 3: Principles of Effective Communication

The art of communication is essential to have for anyone to succeed in any field. People use their communication skills to convey their thoughts, feelings and emotions to others. Although all of us communicate in our own way but very few of us know how to communicate effectively. Just like everything has some principles to follow, effective communication is based on five important principles and it is not possible to excel in this skill without considering these principles.

Listening

Listening is very important in the effective communication as those people who are great listeners, are great communicators actually. If you have the ability to convey your thoughts and ideas in an excellent way that everyone understands and appreciates them but your listening skills are poor, your communication will not be effective at all because you will not be able to get the thoughts and ideas of others completely so, you can't respond to them appropriately. This causes frustration for the speaker and the process of communication becomes very difficult.

Proper listening does not only mean that you understand the words or the information being given by the speaker but it also means that you understand the feelings and emotions which the speaker is trying to convey to the listeners.

Therefore, in order to make your listening effective, you have to pay full attention to enhance these skills. As you improve in this area, your listening will automatically get better and this way you make the speaker enjoy the conversation as they realize that you are getting their each and every point.

Effectiveness

When your communication skills are effective, you can develop good understanding with others. People you interact with will understand you, and you will understand them, and this mutual understanding is something that makes the relationships stronger and long-lasting. You won't need to use manipulation or other tactics to win the hearts of others. This will ultimately result in satisfaction with your management and they will trust you more than others.

Perceptual Filters

Sometimes people speak in certain codes and one has to be aware of them in order to pick everything correctly during the conversation. Different people have different perceptual filters that they use in communication to understand others and convey their thoughts or information.

You should pay attention to how you can learn the perceptual filters of certain people you are in interaction with, so that you can communicate with them in better way. This way there won't be any confusion and you will be able to build a healthy relationship with them.

Patience

Patience is much needed in the effective communication because it takes both time and effort to make others understand your ideas and gain the complete information and sometimes failing to do so puts you in frustration and you want to give up on your intention. At that stage, don't forget that you have to win not to lose, so just keep the positive attitude, try to find the right words to communicate your thoughts and you will ultimately succeed.

You might be failing because the words you were using were not passing through the perceptual filters of the listeners and they were not able to understand you properly.

Relationships

What you can achieve with effective communication is stronger relationship with others.

When you learn and start following the principles of effective communication on daily basis at your work place, you are not far away from achieving your goals. All you have to do is take small steps and practice as much as you can and success will be yours

Chapter 4: How to Communicate Better at the Workplace

Perhaps one of the reasons that effective communication in the workplace is being taken for granted in some workplaces is because some people don't really know what it means. What is effective workplace communication, anyway?

Bosses just send emails to the managers and the managers do the same to the supervisors. The supervisors then just relay important updates to the employees through text messages, Skype chat or some other form of digital communication. In the past, when there was important news to be shared with the workers of a company, the upper management would call for a meeting with the middle management and the middle management would have a meeting with the workers afterward. These days, however, there just isn't time to hold traditional meetings. The speed at which businesses move prevents people from connecting on a personal level, and people have learned to sacrifice face-to-face communication for faster business transactions.

However, effective communication in the workplace is not limited only to the means by which messages are sent.

Being able to communicate better in the workplace is essential for your career. Imagine the stress and failure you'd undergo if you're not able to convey your true thoughts and brilliant ideas. While your colleagues succeed, you're left wallowing in a corner because you can't express your ideas, thoughts, and plans for your company. To assist you in communicating better at your workplace, here are steps you can implement.

Establish Convenient Venues of Communication

As a personnel and part of a team, you have to establish a venue where your colleagues can communicate with you conveniently. You can connect with them online or offline. Having person-to-person communication is, of course, best because you can also interpret any non-verbal language. Let your colleagues know that you're open to communication.

Be Honest and Sincere

You can only become a better communicator if you're honest and sincere. Conveying your message honestly will benefit you too, because you can say what you want without fear because you're honest and sincere. Couple this with diplomacy, though, so that there will be no bad blood between you and your colleagues. You must observe sincerity too, due to the fact that without it, the message you want to convey can fall on deaf ears. Your honesty and sincerity will shine through and your colleagues will trust you more.

Settle Disputes Directly with the Person Concerned

You have to talk to the person concerned first, before anything else. There are many employees who report to higher-ups first, before talking to the person concerned. This is not the proper way to do it. You have to know the other person's side first, and take it from there. Remember to observe honesty, tact, and respect when talking to this person. If he or she shouts, keep calm. If he or she curses, don't curse back. You can't fight fire with fire. Choose the high road instead and you'll end up winning.

Listen More and Talk Less

A great conversationalist listens more and talks less. You can communicate better this way. It's a two-way process that allows you to convey what you want to say. When the person becomes aware that you're not condescending or talking down, he or she will gradually loosen up and listen more to you.

Express Yourself Properly

Be articulate in your language and use brief but exact statements. Tactfulness, of course, is more important than brevity. Whenever you find yourself in a sticky situation, it's better to use more words to be tactful than being brief but rude. Rudeness has no place in good communication. Here are some pointers you can adapt to express yourself properly.

Talk in a normal manner

Don't rush through your words or falter in your speech. Speaking in a normal manner signifies your desire to be heard correctly. Avoid mumbling to yourself.

Maintain the proper distance

This will depend on the person you're talking to. If the individual is a superior, then you can position yourself a comfortable distance away from him or her. If it's a friend, then you can stand closer. Don't let the person misunderstand you just because you've kept an inappropriate distance.

Avoid mannerisms

Focus on the person you're talking to and avoid mannerisms. Don't play with your hair, or bite your fingernails while talking. These actions can be misconstrued negatively.

Listen attentively

Whether you're speaking to a family member or a colleague, you have to listen attentively. What does the individual truly want to say? What's the true meaning of his or her statements?

Show respect

Express yourself to the other person in a respectful manner, and you'll likewise earn the other's respect. You can emphasize a point by speaking calmly and respectfully.

Use simple, understandable language

You have to adjust your language to the level of your receiver. However, you don't have to use highfalutin words to express your ideas. The simpler your language is, the more understandable it is.

Chapter 5: How to Communicate Better at Home

Now, let's take what we've learned and apply it to the home environment with these simple steps:

Keep Communication Lines Open

You can't communicate well if there are no venues open for its fruition. You'll have to allow every member of your family a way to contact you or reach each other. You can use cell phones, emails, tweets, Facebook posts, or snail mail to communicate. Let your family members know where they can reach you promptly. Remember to respond immediately to any form of communication from any member. This way, they'll know that they can keep in touch with you anytime and anywhere, and they'll know they're a priority.

Learn How to Express Yourself Appropriately

Since you know the characteristics of your family members more than anyone else, you should also know how to convey your message properly. If you're talking to a younger person, you can speak as a concerned adult. On the other hand, if you're speaking to another adult, you can talk as an equal so as to avoid sounding condescending.

Strive to speak in a calm manner, even when you're angry, and they'll listen to you.

When you're angry, don't immediately open your mouth. Instead, take time to relax or to take deep breaths first before saying anything. There are three things you can never get back in this world: lost opportunities, time mis-spent, and ill-spoken words. Sometimes, hurtful words are even more destructive than physical wounds because they leave deep scars that time cannot always heal.

Settle Differences Before the Sun Sets

Allowing differences to go unsettled at the end of the day will oftentimes lead to prolonged misunderstandings. You must do your best to settle misunderstandings within the day. They're your family – your loved ones - and time is short. Who knows what could happen the following day? Too many people only realize the importance of their families after it's too late. Don't be among them. Be a better communicator by expressing yourself promptly and clearly.

Dialogue with Your Family

Don't assume that since they're family, they will understand everything you say or do. You have to spend time with your family. This may be in a leisurely manner or for pure dialogue. You can combine both leisure and dialogue. In fact, this is an ideal venue where you can interact with each other. Whatever the activity is, you must talk to your family; not a meaningless chatter, but a heart-to-heart talk with them. If you haven't spoken to one member of your family in a long time, now is the time to mend your fences and communicate.

Show by Example, Not by Words

You can always say you're a better communicator than anyone else in your family, but you should demonstrate this through your actions and not through your words. How? By talking to them properly. Show them that when you communicate, you pay attention to the person you're talking to. Make direct eye contact with them, and don't multitask during your conversation. Treat them with respect and love. Don't hold shouting bouts with them. Speak clearly, calmly, and honestly and in a tactful manner. You can motivate your family members to join you in your quest to have open communication within your family.

Respect Each Member

When you respect the person you're talking to, he or she will have to show respect to you too. No matter how rude an individual is, he or she will react to your positive action. Don't react to that individual's rudeness by becoming rude yourself. Why should you change your good character based on the negative action of one family member? You have to motivate that person, instead, to follow your lead and in turn show others some respect too.

Be Honest but Diplomatic

Say what you honestly want to say in a diplomatic manner. This is also one way of showing respect. As previously discussed, you can be honest by expressing what you feel about the other person without attacking him or her; especially when that person you're talking to is someone you love.

Pay Attention to Non-Verbal Language

Listen attentively when you talk with your loved ones. Observe the person's non-verbal language. You can understand a person better if you're aware of his or her body language. A number of lonely persons, drug addicts, and persons with suicidal tendencies were saved because of a relative's accurate interpretation of non-verbal cues. In addition, you can also strengthen a bond when you can have sincere and focused communication with your family members.

Establish a Communication System within the Family

You can create a communication system within your family where there can be a hierarchy of action. Once this system is in place, it has to be implemented diligently. An example is during emergencies; the first person to be contacted – aside from 911– can be the parents, then the older siblings, and then the younger ones.

You can communicate better at home when you

follow these effective steps. Your initial action may not be successful, but keep going. Eventually, through your constant effort to communicate better, other family members will catch on too and emulate your example. Soon, not only you, but your whole family will benefit from your diligence and determination.

Chapter 6: Build Trust with Effective Communication

Trust is hard to earn these days partly because of rampant bad behavior but also because of poor communication. Even in this day and age when there are more means and methods for communication, people fail to keep up with the changes. Instead of improving communication skills and using it to inspire loyalty and build trust, the means are at times the reasons why the skill deteriorates.

To succeed in today's age of "Me" generation and stiffer competition, you need to be a good communicator. If not, others who are more assertive will get ahead of you. Key relationships are also hard to come by without effective communication fostering deeper connection and trust. Though communication is largely about conveying information, ideas, thoughts, messages and news, you also have to remember that it is also partly about building trust.

Now you may ask, how do you build trust through

communication? Here's how:

Understand what matters to others

Whether with your personal, business or work relationships, one of the best ways to build trust is to know what matters to them. When communicating with other people, you need to turn on your perceptiveness meter. When they know you care about what matters to them, trust is a likely by product.

Listen actively and intently

Listening as part of effective communication couldn't be reiterated more. If you want trust, you need to balance be an expert of both sides of the process. Just look how telephones - one of today's primary means of communicating - work. It has part for talking and for listening which tells you exactly what you should. When you're done taking, give the other person the spotlight and while doing so listen actively to build better connection.

Match words with actions

Just like you need to sync body language with words to facilitate effective communication, you also need to match your words with actions if you want to build trust through communication. When words are backed up by actions and people see that you are a person of your word, credibility is established. And as you more likely already know, credibility is a critical element of trust.

Share opinions with an open mind

You may be an expert of communication but no matter how good you are, you should know that there are always people who will not agree with you. When you share your opinion, tell it like it is an opinion and not an idea you are shoving down on other people's throats.

As the saying goes, respect begets respect. If you can respect other people's opinions even if disagreements exist, fostering trust is going to be easy. After all, trust is not based on whether people like you or your opinion. It's about you respecting others and getting the same in return.

Be honest at all times

While there are instances when information cannot be shared, you still need to live by one of life's golden rules - be honest at all times and expect the same thing in return. Regardless of whom you are talking or interacting with, honesty always come a long way. If you're someone who values and hones integrity, you can definitely expect greater trust in every aspect of your life.

Chapter 7: Mindset for effective communication

Before we begin our journey into critical conversations the first thing that we need to look at and master is our mindset. What most people don't know, realize or accept is that our mind is the most underused and most understood organ in the human body. With our minds we can accomplish anything that we can possibly imagine as well as limit ourselves to the most basic of tasks and possibilities.

When it comes to mindset it all comes down to what it is that you want and what you are willing to do or not do to achieve it. When looking at mindset, look at it as a coin. On one side we have everything that we want and desire whereas on the other side of the coin we have all of the excuses and issues that prevent us from achieving our goals. For the majority of us however we walk the edge of the coin looking down at the shiny side of our hopes and desires while favoring or listening to the doubts and echoes from the other side.

Your Self Image

The next layer of our mindset can be found in our self-image. The way that we look at ourselves and the way we perceive others looking at us is a major factor in our mindset and the actions that we engage. For instance, if you are someone who is overweight, doesn't speak well, has a disability or just doesn't feel right physically or emotionally your self-image will be affected by this. One the other side of the coin if you are slender, well educated, has a lot of friends and is healthier than ever your self-image will be greater resulting in more positive outcomes and conversations.

Knowing your abilities and limitations

The third level of mindset is our personal knowledge and understanding of our abilities and limitations. To stat this off I want to first say that no one is perfect. However, if you know that you are not perfect and can accept that you have limitations then you have the foundation to build form and grow.

When we know and accept our limitations we can better position ourselves into situations that we feel comfortable and in control. If we feel comfortable and in control we are more likely to be in a better frame of mind to have more intelligent conversations with our inner voices. If however, we find ourselves in situations that we are not comfortable in it is our job to restructure our mindsets to work in a positive way. And we can do this with critical conversations.

You are an island among many

The final component in regards to mindset is one that is seldom talked about or referred to. This is the knowledge that you are an island among many. What this basically means is that you are responsible for you first and foremost. Where many of us fall into the mindset trap is that we think of others first instead of ourselves. Now, I am not saying that you need to be selfish and self-centered. What I am saying is that at the end of the day when all of the kids are asleep, you are lying there in bed wide awake staring at the ceiling letting the events of the day fill your mind just know that you are one with yourself.

The actions that you perform or fail to perform will ultimately affect you in the end. Your kids will one day go off to school, your spouse may divorce you, you may lose or find another job, get a new house, car or win the lottery or eventually die. It is when we find ourselves in these situations we really begin to have these critical conversations with ourselves. Knowing how we plan to handle these conversations when they arrive will ultimately determine their outcomes.

Chapter 8: How to Communicate Effectively at Work

If there was ever a place where communication skills mattered the most, it is in the workplace. If you can master the ability to communicate effectively with not just your colleagues, but your superiors, managers and all staff levels in every industry, you are in a position of power because you hold one of the most valuable skills an employee can possess.

Even though we live in a digital age where the majority of our work is conducted online, over the phones, emails or even through social media (as a lot of companies tend to do their marketing these days), effective communication skills are still a prized asset that is not going to go away anytime soon. Aside from being able to communicate well to survive in everyday life, there is one other scenario in which effective communication is a crucial skill that you are going to need if you want to succeed – the workplace. Whether you work in a team or if your profession requires you to interact with customers and clients daily, certain situations can be challenging to handle. Without the right communication skills, it can be even more of a challenge. Imagine trying to persuade a dissatisfied client without being able to properly convey the message that you want. You could just end up putting the client off even more and put yourself at risk of losing their business if they have a hard time understanding what you are trying to say. Do you see how important being able to communicate well is?

How to Improve Communication Skills at the Workplace?

The most successful people who eventually go on to become leaders and managers in the workplace are the ones who can make great impressions on everyone they work with because of how well they communicate. Of course, being able to do the job well does play a part of it as well, but when you can meaningfully and effectively communicate with the people you work with, you are already halfway towards success.

At work, we are required to communicate a lot more than we normally would in our everyday lives. We're communicating with clients, with colleagues, with managers, with bosses, through emails, over the phone and even during meetings and presentations.

Improve Your Body Language

Body language is applicable in the workplace too, perhaps even more so because this is where it really matters. At work, the way you carry yourself and communicate is just as important as how well you get the job done. Remember how our nonverbal cues can speak volumes even when we don't say a word? So, while at work, always adopt confident body language whenever you step into your workplace. Do not slouch, do not fold or cross your arms, do not frown or look sullen. Always be positive, and project a warm and welcoming manner, smile and make eye contact with the people you pass by.

Avoid Over-Communicating

Avoid being long-winded and beating around the bush when you have discussions and conversations at work. You may think you are trying to be as effective as possible by communicating every little detail, even what is seemingly unnecessary, but avoid doing that because there is such a thing as over-communicating. Even in presentations, droning on for too long puts you at risk of losing the attention span of your audience. The best way to communicate effectively is to be brief, concise and only communicate what is necessary and relevant to the situation or discussion at hand.

Seek Feedback

The best way to know if you are effective in what you do, or if what you are doing is working, is to seek feedback honest feedback from your colleagues. Regularly seeking feedback will help you discover what areas you should be working on to improve, and often it is others who can shed better perspective on the things that we may overlook.

Engage with Your Audience

If you are tasked with presenting at a meeting, this is a great way for you to put into practice your effective communication skills. Now, business presentations are not the most riveting topic, and attention spans will drift eventually, so what do effective communicators do? They engage with their audience. Being effective in your communication requires that you can deliver the points you want to say to an audience that is paying attention. During the meeting or presentation, ask questions and encourage your audience to respond and share their points of view.

Watching Your Tone of Voice

At the workplace, you need to always ensure that your tone is professional yet friendly and welcoming at the same time. Sometimes it may be necessary to be assertive to stand firm on a point, but still, try and maintain a professional tone when you do that to avoid coming off as aggressive. Effective communication at work requires that you be able to master being confident, direct, professional yet calm and cooperative at the same time.

Checking Your Grammar

This step is applicable for emails and written communication at the workplace. The most effective communicators are ones who can write flawlessly with no mistakes because they put in the extra effort to check and proofread everything that they type or write before they hit the send button. Check it twice, check it thrice, check it as many times as you need to ensure everything is completely on point before it gets sent. You will impress everyone with your perfect grammar and punctuation, and the ones who read your emails will be able to understand what you are trying to say just as if you were standing there in front of them talking to them.

Speaking with Clarity

Good communication means being able to be easily understood by everyone you speak to. Practice being able to put forth the messages that you want to say is as few and concise words as possible, this will help you speak with clarity because you already know exactly what needs to be said. Preparing your talking points ahead of time is another great way to boost speech clarity and keep the conversation fillers to a minimum. It also helps avoid excessive and unnecessary talking about irrelevant points, because you want your receiver to be clear about the message, not walk away from the discussion still feeling more confused about it.

Practice Friendliness

Would you enjoy speaking to someone who is unfriendly and stand-offish at the office? The obvious answer would be no. Nobody would want to engage in a conversation because they would be put off by the person's very demeanor even before they have said a word. To become an effective communicator at work, you need to start adopting a friendly and approachable persona which will encourage your co-workers to want to approach you and have a conversation with you. A friendly approach is even more important when you are having a face-to-face discussion, especially if you are in a managerial position because your colleagues aren't going to want to open up to you if they feel intimidated even before the discussion has properly begun.

Be Confident

Being confident is an important part of becoming an effective communicator overall. When you interact with others around you at the workplace, the moment you show you are confident you will find it much easier to hold effective conversations with your colleagues and team members that will result in things getting done. Why? Because they are drawn towards your confident approach. Confident people are not thwarted by challenges, they rise to meet them, and this is what people at work want to follow.

Say No to Distractions

Meeting rooms exist in the workplace for a reason, and its time to make full use of them. The best way to have a meaningful conversation with the people you work with is to keep the distractions to a minimum. In an environment like work where so many people are working in close proximity with one another, phones can be constantly ringing off the hook, people will be on the move walking up and down, and several conversations could be going on at once. Not exactly the most conducive environment to hold a discussion, much less an effective conversation. Keep the distractions to a minimum, go into a meeting room and close the door, put the phones away and then when both parties are ready, begin your conversation.

Keep Your Points Consistent

To be able to deliver messages effectively means you need to be able to remain on point and consistent with what you are saying. It helps if you stick to the facts and the focus of the discussion at hand, write down and prepare your talking points before you hold the conversation. Your points should flow smoothly, and nothing should contradict each other because you could end up confusing the receiver of your message and they become unsure about what it is you are trying to say. Your key points of your message are also at risk of being lost when you contradict yourself far too much. Plan and prepare ahead, make some notes and have them ready if you need to refer to them to help you stay on course. This is how you practice becoming a more effective communicator.

Remain as Transparent as Possible

There is nothing that is disliked more at the workplace than a lack of transparency. Never try to hide information, or leave out bits and pieces of information when working with your colleagues on a project or working in a team. It makes it difficult for everyone involved to communicate well if they don't have all the necessary information on hand to work with.

Why effective communication matters in the workplace

Effective Communication Forms and Maintains Relationships and Rapport

At the workplace, it is important to maintain positive and amicable relationships with your co-workers. You are going to spend most your day working together with them, and without the proper communication skills on hand, it can be difficult to build and construct productive relationships with the ones you work with.

Effective Communication Promotes Innovation

Innovation at the workplace increases when its employees are comfortable and confident enough to openly communicate their ideas and work well with one another. When employees are not able to communicate their exact thoughts and ideas, or if they don't feel confident enough to do so, the chances of good ideas ever being implemented in the workplace become slim to none.

Effective Communication Builds Better Teamwork

When effective communication flows freely in the workplace, it is easier to build teams which are productive and cohesive, who work well together to get things done. When employees within a team can communicate and get along well with one another, the staff morale is given a boost because they feel confident in what they are during. When the management communicates the company's mission and vision effectively, the employees will turn feel more secure in their roles and be able to perform better as a result. Work ethics are also improved when internal communication within a company is excellent because the staff fully understand what common goal it is that they are working towards.

Effective Communication Can Boost the Growth of the Company

A company relies on effective marketing to generate business and sales. Marketing is about delivering strong messages across to the clients, making sure that those messages hit the target right where they are supposed to. How is this done? By relying on effective communication. Communication, especially in the marketing role, is crucial because, without the great marketing collateral, good communication internally and externally becomes a struggle for the company. When the company starts to struggle, it is only a matter of time before it folds because it is not able to work to overcome those barriers.

Effective Communication Helps Promote Transparency

Transparency at the workplace is important to help build trust in the brand. This trust must be gained both internally among the employees, and externally among the clients. Transparency and effective communication go hand-in-hand because when it comes time for tough decisions to be made, the company leaders will have a much easier time explaining why to their employees if they practice effective communication.

Effective Communication Will Boost Customer Service

If you are going to provide top-notch service to your clients, you are going to need to be able to understand what they want. Exactly what they want. If you don't, there is no way you are going to be able to meet their needs or even go the extra mile to deliver the best service you possibly can. No matter what you may be selling, your relationship with your clients relies heavily on your ability to be able to communicate effectively, because you need to be able to convince them why they should go along with your business instead of your competitors.

Chapter 9: How to communicate effectively with Kids

To start you on your journey in critical communications we are going to talk about kids. For most of us kids aren't really looked upon as people who we have deep and meaningful conversations with. In fact, most people will look at children as needing to be educated and told what to do rather than sit down with them and have a meaningful conversation.

Yes, it is true that there are topics and subject depending on the age rage of the child you may not be able to talk to them about or if you did they may not have the mental or emotional maturity to understand and react to the conversation but as a whole child are pretty smart, are extremely creative and uninfluenced by the adult baggage we carry with us.

What is their age?

When adjusting your mindset, you need to look at the age of the child. In today's day and age, it seems that children are growing up and turning into adults at five and six years of age but the truth is that they are still children and they need to be addressed as children.

Understanding of the world

What is their understanding of the world? With the introduction of the Internet and its wide spread acceptance and use in our day to day lives it is getting to be harder and harder to shield our children from these things as we once did. In today's world our children can find out pretty much anything that they want to know with a simple Google search.

As such it is critical that we understand their understanding of the world. With so much misinformation and conflicting information it is easy for them to become confused and form their own opinion on the world. When communication with children it is very important that you listen to them, watch what they do and educate yourself on their world so that it is much easier for you to communicate with them in theirs.

Educate yourself and them

In the education process of communication with children you as the parent need to educate yourself to their world. One of the most important aspect of this education will be their language. Throughout time starting back in the 1960's or so children began to come up with phrases, terms and their own universal language that makes perfect sense to them but is a foreign tongue to the rest of us.

When we were growing up the word "Cool" meant one thing and ten years later the word "Bad" means just the opposite. It is the constant shifting of these words, meanings and global understanding that makes communication so difficult.

You can begin to understand the context to their conversations and begin to pull our red flags that as a parent you will want to be aware of. From there you will want to start observing and monitoring their body language and communications. Now, I am not saying to go out there and spy on your kids or install Nanny Software on your kids computers but I am saying if you want to learn how to communicate with your kids or children in general it is important that you educate yourself with the same material that they are educating themselves with.

Lead by example

When it comes to communication with children words might not be the best way to get your point and meaning across. Again, depending on the age and emotional maturity of those you are talking to these actions may not fit but if you use actions over words then you may have a better communication medium to turn to.

When dealing with children not all children will do what you want them to do. In fact, the odds are they will probably do the opposite. So, what are you to do in order to get them to change their mindset to reflect yours?

The first thought would be to sit them down and talk

to them like an adult. Again, they are not adults and trying to move them up into your position as an adult and expect them to understand is harder and less effective than other options. The next thought or option that many will turn to is punishment. To start with people will send their kids to their rooms, take away privileges. On the surface this seems like a good way to gain control and teach someone a lesson when in fact it just shuts down the lines of communication which in turn pushes people away from each other.

The final action that people will use for communication is physical and emotional abuse or intimidation. This is a tactic that should never be used and in fact destroys all lines of communication since those being abused will just shut down and do whatever it takes to keep things away from their abuser out of fear.

Be Patient

When it comes to communicating with children it is important that you be patient. You need to understand and adjust your mindset, education and actions according to each specific situation. Remembering and understanding this will go a long way to keeping the line of communication open.

Keeping the lines of communication open

And finally the best way to communicate with a child and anyone for that matter is to create a secure and welcoming environment. If we let children know that we are always there to talk, have proven that they can talk to us on a wide range of subject and that they won't get physically or emotionally abused then communication becomes that much easier.

Chapter 10: Effective communication in relationship

Divorce across the world is rapidly becoming a multi-billion-dollar business. In fact, ins the United States divorce is almost as popular and even as widely celebrated as weddings. When a couple gets married the entire world looks bright and filled with possibilities. Typically, those who get married in their early twenties, are just getting out of school, finding bright promising new jobs and in their minds nothing can go wrong. Unfortunately, just like with all things in life something will always go wrong somewhere along the way. And how you and your partner deal with these situations will ultimately determine the health and well-being of this marriage.

The Lines of Communication

When entering into a lifelong partnership with another individual there has to be a specific bond that transcends everything else. This is the mindset layer of communications. When we get married it is considered to be a union of both body and soul. At the end what is yours is mine and what's mine is yours. This needs to be the foundation of a marriage if it is going to work.

As such the lines of communication are critical in expressing this understanding. Once the lines of communication are broken down there is little or no chance to repair them.

Emotional health

It is important that each party feel physically and emotionally safe. They need to know that if an issue needs to be discussed that it can be discussed and worked on. If at any time the emotional health of your partner is weakened it will take some time to recover if at all.

This is why it is important to build trust in your relationship before even entering into marriage. I am talking about a deeper trust that can only be found in a marriage.

Keeping Secrets

When it comes to keeping secrets there are two sides to the coin. There is the side of the coin where you shouldn't keep secrets from your partner and the other side where you shouldn't be spreading secrets to others.

When we keep secrets form our partners we are doing much more damage than we would if we just kept the lines of communication open. If for example, we tell our spouse that we don't like their cooking then we may make them feel bad for a short period of time. If we don't tell them that we don't like their cooking we may end up eating crap meals that they believe we enjoy.

Keeping secrets from others

When we are in relationships with others there will be many times that things are said and done that we feel are harmless and could be told to others when in reality they are very embarrassing and could either cause emotional or other harm. This is where our education about the emotional health of others comes into play.

For example, if your spouse tells you a secret about a co-worker or even just a story about something that happened at work and you happen to mention it to someone else who in turn tells someone else and this information gets back to the person the story was about then this puts your spouse in an awkward position where trust has been broken.

When your spouse gets home that night they may be upset at you for telling a story that was told to you in confidence. Now, it may not have been stated outright that this information was confidential or that you shouldn't tell another about it, but rather it was implied due to the bonds of your relationship.

This is where communication and understanding of your unspoken language is critical. If the lines of communication are broken or message and meanings are not spoken plain as day situations like these will occur on a regular basis.

Developing rules of behavior

When in a relationship it is vital that you develop rules of behavior and have a clear understanding of these rules and their consequences if they are broken. In the above example it would be a good rule to state that anything that is talked about in the bedroom or talked about alone should never be talked about in public. If this rule is broken both parties should understand that unforeseen consequences may occur.

Joking around isn't a joke

When working on the emotional health of your partner joking around may do more damage than intended. As adults we have very little time for fun and enjoyment. Our days are typically filled with dealing with the kids, working a long job, paying bills and other non-exciting activities.

When we do find time to let our hair down and have fun jokes, funny stories and pranks may occur. When it comes to your spouse however you may want to think twice and even three times before pulling that prank or saying the punchline. This is why you need to setup boundaries and guidelines that you can follow so these jokes don't turn into arguments.

Have nightly or weekly meetings

When it comes to communication having a meeting might sound stupid or embarrassing. The truth is however when you setup a time to have a family meeting or if you are just a couple without kids, a date night meeting where a safe environment is created you can more easily get problems and thoughts off your chest and resolved before they grow and pile on.

Just communicate

In conclusion many people believe that the reasons for divorce in this country is the lack of money. This is not the reason. The reason for divorce is the lack of communication or waiting too long to start communicating. The sooner you start and the less concern you have on the feelings of others the more likely you can fix problems before they occur.

Chapter 11: Benefits of Effective Communication

Communication, quite simply, is defined as the exchanging of information that we do amongst ourselves and other individuals.

If you live in this world, you need to relate to others around you. Nobody can survive without having their needs met, and to have our needs met, whether we like it or not, requires the help of other individuals to do so. And therefore, we need to rely on communication to get by.

Communication is a skill that many don't think twice about, but it is one of the most important skills you could have at your disposal. If you want to know what it is like not to be able to communicate or be understood, just picture a time when you have gone to a foreign country where you do not speak the local language.

Everything suddenly becomes more difficult, doesn't it? You struggle to understand and to make yourself understood, and even simple forms of communication like asking for directions seems like an impossible task. Communication, both verbal and nonverbal, matters. It matters because it helps us relate and collaborate with the people living in the world with us.

Helps Express Ideas & Pass Information

Think of all the greatest inventions that we have in our lives today. All of those came to fruition because the inventors were able to communicate their brilliant ideas to the rest of the world. Effective communication is the reason people can facilitate the process of information and knowledge sharing so seamlessly. Without it, a lot of our ideas, thoughts, and points of view would just be trapped inside our head, and we would not know what to do about it. If you can effectively master the art of communication and make it easy for people to understand, your chances of conveying the information without the danger of being completely misinterpreted will increase that much more.

Messages are Conveyed Clearly

The receiver understands you and your message. There will be fewer misunderstandings because people in your workplace and at home will not misconstrue your words. Your intended meaning is conveyed.

Increased Frequency of Conflicts

Many people don't mean what they say and do. They're just unfamiliar with the proper way of relaying their thoughts, ideas, and emotions. If a person doesn't take time to hone his communication skills, he'll most likely get sucked into conflicts, which could have been easily avoided. Many arguments are actually unnecessary because they just stemmed from the wrong tone of voice or wrong choice of words. Further, lack of eye contact and inappropriate gestures can also turn a peaceful conversation into an exchange of horrible words.

One of the main elements of good communication is respect between two conversing sides. If respect is not shown, then ill reactions will certainly ensue. Whether you're talking with a family member, friend, or a colleague, it's always necessary to communicate with respect. Decrease the frequency of conflicts and avoid getting into a heated argument with anyone by learning how to use words and gestures well.

Better Relationships

Your relationships will improve because you can express yourself well. Your family and coworkers will surely appreciate an honest and sincere person around them. When you know how to express yourself honestly without inflicting harm, then your relationships will significantly improve.

Improved Communication Skills

You're able to correctly say what you want to say and in a diplomatic manner. You can express your thoughts honestly but tactfully. You know how to interpret body language and relate it to what the other person is saying. You'll learn how to maintain a good conversation without batting an eyelash.

Less Stress

When you know that you're able to express yourself freely without hurting someone unintentionally, you'll be less stressed and less anxious. The fear of being unable to communicate properly and saying the right things are major sources of stress and anxiety. This can cause you to always be on your toes, wary of instances that would force you to communicate with other people.

A Healthier Life

Do you know that stress is the root cause of a number of diseases such as hypertension, hyperacidity, and cardiac disease? In Virginia, numerous studies have proven this fact already. Less stress and anxiety, in turn, will lead to a healthier life.

A More Successful and Happy Life

When your relationships at home and in your workplace are improved due to your improved communication skills, your endeavors are more likely to succeed as well. Everyone will strive to cooperate with you to achieve your goals. This will allow you to lead a happier life.

These are the benefits you can attain when you communicate better. Communication serves a crucial part of your daily life and you have to strive to develop it if you want to go through life like a winner.

Reduces Misunderstanding

We all know what happens when information is misunderstood or taken out of context. Heated arguments arise, fights happen, and sometimes relationships get severed because misunderstood information causes hurt feelings or hit a sore spot with someone. That is another major reason why effective communication is such a vital skill to possess. You exist in this world; you need to be able to express your messages clearly and to the point to minimize the chances that what you are going to say is going to cause problems for yourself and the people that you are speaking to.

Effective Communication Increases Your Confidence

That's because they're able to communicate well. When you can communicate effectively, your self-esteem and confidence level rise because you do not doubt at all that you can express and tell people exactly what you want them to know. When you can communicate well, you find that you are no longer shy and awkward when it comes time for you to speak, because you know exactly what to do and how to handle the situation.

Effective Communication Will Help You Go Far

If you want to be successful at everything you do in life, you need to confidently be able to communicate effectively, because this is how you are going to set yourself apart from the rest. Do you notice how the most successful people in the world are the ones who can communicate effortlessly?

Chapter 12: Common Barriers Which Prevent Effective Communication

Messages may not come across or be received in the way that we intended, which is why it is important to understand the causes of communication barriers and what can be done to overcome them.

During the communication process, there are sometimes barriers which tend to come up that can result in poor communication. These are known as communication barriers, and these are the reasons your messages become misunderstood, taken out of context or even distorted. To overcome these communication barriers, you must first understand what they are.

Here's a list of some common communication barriers which occur frequently:

Language Differences

Different languages come with different accents, and sometimes, difficulty understanding a person's accent can also be a communication barrier. Perhaps they may be pronouncing certain words differently, or the way their sentences run together may be difficult to understand because of a thick accent for example.

Making Assumptions

A common communication barrier, this frequently occurs when someone decides to reach a decision or course of action without fully listening to all the information at hand. Making assumptions can lead to complications because when you are not well informed, you run the risk of making more mistakes than you should.

Lack of Attention

Not paying full attention is considered a communication barrier. Sometimes, our mind tends to wander or drift when someone else is talking. Or we may be the ones who are doing the talking, but we run the risk of losing the other person's interest because the topic doesn't rivet them enough. When attention starts to drift, it can be easy to miss crucial points in the message.

Current Emotional State

There may be times when it isn't necessarily the best time to bring up a certain subject or topic of discussion. Emotions such as sadness, anger, nervousness, distraction or frustration can hamper the way messages are communicated or received. If someone is not in the right frame of mind or state to pay full attention to what you have to say, they may not be able to process that message appropriately.

A Lack of Confidence

Lacking confidence is also viewed as a communication barrier. When a speaker lacks the necessary confidence needed, they become shy and find it difficult to assert themselves properly, making it difficult to convey messages or make their opinions known. Lacking confidence can result in a lot of awkward pauses, stammering, and stuttering, which could garble the messages and prevent them from being communicated effectively.

Rushing Through the Message

Never convey messages in a rushed or hasty manner. Doing this puts you at risk of missing out crucial information that needs to be communicated, and your listener could miss out on possible information too because they're unable to keep up with what you may be saying. Rushing through messages is never a good idea unless you have the time to spare for a proper discussion, don't do it.

Talking Unnecessarily

Effective communication skills are a powerful tool that anyone can use to achieve success in both personal and professional life. Most common obstacle in communication many people face is unnecessary talk as no one likes to have conversation with the person who talks excessively and irrelevantly.

In order to overcome this obstacle, you have to

analyze your thoughts in your mind before you share with others so that you can talk to the point and everyone understands you easily.

Being Prejudiced

A very harmful element that not only breaks the team spirit but also destroys the environment of healthy competition is Prejudice. When you are prejudiced, you are not willing to pay attention to what is being said and you don't understand it at all.

In order to overcome this obstacle in communication, you have to treat the speaker respectfully and value their opinion and thoughts about whatever they are speaking, regardless of negative things associated with them. Try to bring change in your thinking with positive mindset that their knowledge is the most important thing to you and nothing else.

Distractions

There are four kinds of distractions that may arise as an obstacle in communication and those are mental, physical, auditory and visual distractions. One has to be aware of all of such distractions so the process of communication is not hindered and everything is done smoothly.

Thinking Others Are Imitating You

It's true that some people don't use their mind as much as they should and copy other's ideas and thoughts in their opinions. But it's not necessary that it happens everywhere.

You have to keep your thinking positive and try to learn one important thing that others are not stealing your thoughts but they are sharing their own unique beliefs and values. It is also possible that their suggestions might show a way out of the situations you never got a chance to handle before.

Lack of Confidence

When you can't understand the words or sentences of the speaker correctly at any stage, you are not able to grasp the idea completely and this thing will be a big obstacle for you in communication. You might be afraid that it is not appropriate to tell the speaker that you did not get their point because it can be a bad impression in your perspective but this is not the case at all.

You can feel free to let them know what you are not clear about and they will be happy to clarify their words for your better understanding. They will take it positively and appreciate that you are taking deep interest in whatever is being said.

Improper Way of Interruption

You leave a bad impression on others when you interrupt the speaker with wrong body language or words and this can be a big obstacle in effective communication.

In order to overcome this barrier, you must listen with patience and wait for some pause. When you get a chance, use a decent body language like raising your arm, saying sorry for the interruption and putting your query in front of them very politely.

Absence of Mind

Trying to fake the attention is what many people do when they are not taking interest in the conversation. Although they are having the proper eye contact with the speaker but their mind is diverted to something else. This thing not only creates an obstacle in communication but also shows disrespectful attitude of the listener towards the speaker.

Try to focus your attention at the speaker with the thought that he or she has got some important knowledge and ideas that you really need to know about. You can keep a notebook with you and write down important points of the conversation. This practice will help you improve your attention span and focus, prevent your mind from getting diverted. This way you won't need to fake your attention during the conversation.

Emotions

Getting emotional during the conversation hinders the communication and one can't understand the speaker properly because during the emotions of anger or sadness our senses can't function at the required level and we are not able to stay focused at the speaker's words.

Noisy Environment

Noise is one of the most common environmental barriers in communication. When there is noisy environment, nothing can be understood during the conversation and it's a waste of time for everyone. The best thing to do is to hold the conversation as far away from the noisy place as possible.

Other options are trying to reduce the noise by switching off the appliances that are creating the noise and talking to people or kids causing the noise that they should choose some other place for their activity.

Fear Factor

One very important factor that does not let you have effective communication is fear. When you have fear of something in your mind, you can't stay engaged in the conversation. You have to defeat that fear by one way or the other, so that you can keep yourself calm. In order to do this, you should take deep breadths and try to make your mind free from all the negative thoughts coming from outside.

Chapter 13: How to Overcome Communication Barriers

Now that you know the type of barriers which can occur that prevent effective communication from happening, here comes the next question. How do we overcome these barriers?

Take Steps to Clarify

To help improve the effectiveness of your message going across, spend sometimes clarifying the message that you want to communicate before you communicate it. If it helps, write down what you want to say, it makes it easier to assess your message when you see it written down in front of you. To help you determine if your message is clear enough, ask yourself is the objective of the message clear, ask yourself if you are getting all the important information across, and analyze which aspect of the message could be misunderstood and what can you do to prevent that from happening.

Communicate with Your Receiver in Mind

Messages sometimes need to be adjusted and tweaked a little bit depending on whom you are talking to. Remember that people tend to process information differently? You wouldn't necessarily communicate a certain message to your boss the same way that you would to your colleague or a friend. The way you talk and your approach would be completely different. When preparing to communicate, to ensure that your message is the most effective, you need to structure and prepare it according to who is going to receive the message. Making it easier to understand for the receiver improves your chances of that message being communicated effectively.

Keep the Language and Tone in Mind

When attempting to communicate your messages, you – as the communicator – need to ensure that you frame those messages in a clear, easy to understand language. You also need to be aware of the tone you use to deliver that message. Ideally, it should be in a manner that will not risk offending or injuring the feelings of the receiver. The language used to deliver those messages should also be kept brief, concise and to the point, avoid using unnecessary jargon or technical terms where possible because those could just overcomplicate things.

Keep Your Messages Consistent

When communicating, you need to take extra measures to ensure that your messages remain consistent and your points don't contradict each other. What you are trying to convey should be consistent and with a clear focus in mind, so as not to confuse your recipient. When communicating at work, ensure that your messages are clearly in line with company's objectives, mission, and policies, so your colleagues or employees are clear on what needs to be done.

Listening Effectively

Being able to listen effectively is also part of the effective communication process. Both the communicator and the receiver must be able to listen effectively to one another while each is expressing their points of view. Relevant and important information is in danger of being missed if you are not able to listen well to what the communicator is trying to say to you. And in the case of the communicator, they would also need to be able to listen to the feedback that they are receiving if they hope to improve their communication skills moving forward.

Minimize Distraction

To avoid your messages being lost in translation, finding a good place where you can conduct a discussion is going to be your best bet. The less the distraction, the higher the chances of improved concentration and focus when a discussion is taking place, thereby improving effective communication.

Using the Right Word Selection

Word selection is important in determining how effective your messages come across. Words are the source of facilitating effective communication, and careless or improper use of words are usually the reason for poor communication. To improve the effectiveness of your communication, start by carefully considering the types of words used in delivering your message. Minimize the use of jargons, slangs and overly technical terms which may not necessarily be understood by your receiver.

Avoid Inflicting an Air of Superiority

Whether you are discussing with your friends or your co-workers, even if you feel that you are well versed and more knowledgeable about the subject at hand, do not inflict an air of superiority when you are having a discussion. Be relatable and talk to your receiver like an equal, because this helps them be more receptive and attentive to the things you have to say.

Using Visuals

This step is more appropriate for meetings or presentations conducted at work. Instead of droning on and on, at risk of losing the attention of your audience, try including some message-related visuals into your presentation. Not only will this help break the monotony, but you will continue to hold the attention of your audience, improving the chances of your message getting across.

Communication barriers will happen from time to time, whether we like it or not. Whether in everyday life or the workplace, effective communication makes a difference in the way you convey yourself and how easily you are understood by others around you. The way it works is simple – the easier you are to understand, the better your chances of achieving success in whatever task you are undertaking at the moment.

The best thing to do in this instance to prevent the message from being misunderstood or distorted is to be aware of the situation in which you are holding your communication session, and you your best to minimize the efforts wherever possible. Effective communication is possible, once you have a better understanding of what you can do to encourage it.

Chapter 14: Effective Conflict Resolution Communication

Leadership and conflict go hand-in-hand. However, the clinching factor here is how you deal with the conflict. There are plenty of areas in our interpersonal and work life where we deal with conflicts on a daily basis. Think of promotions, salary disputes, personal differences, low appreciation, and other issues. Each time there's a conflict in your business or workplace, you don't have to go running to find another job or business. Instead, be proactive, confront the issue, and remember to avoid personalizing it. Here are a few ways to deal with conflict like a pro.

Try to identify a few common grounds

Even in the most intense conflicts or major differences, there will be something in common with the other party. If nothing else, you both can agree that there is a problem that needs to be resolved. Identify something that you both agree upon, and take off from there. For instance, if you feel like the other person is constantly overpowering you, you both have clear problems there.

Split responsibilities on how each one can tackle their side of the issues to mutually arrive at a solution for the conflict. Say something like "I am sure you are as eager to resolve this as I am. Let us find some solutions we both can agree on to move ahead." You aren't blaming the other person. Rather than making it a battle or competition, you are focusing on arriving at a solution as a team or in collaboration.

If you've made a mistake, promptly offer an apology instead of trying to underplay it. Express regret and accept your mistakes. This doesn't imply you are solely responsible for the problem. It just means that you are accepting your share of the blame to encourage others to follow suit. For instance, "I apologize for uttering those hurtful words. I was angry and upset with what you did.

Tips for giving negative feedback or criticism

While the sandwich method (juxtaposing a negative feedback or criticism between two compliments or positive statements) can be wonderful when it comes to offering feedback or criticism in personal relationships, it may not be very effective in professional scenarios. It may give the worker or employee a false sense of accomplishment, instead of the constructive reality check. If they receive two positive statements, they are likelier to believe they are performing well on the whole. They will most likely take back the compliment rather than criticism, thus preventing further action when it comes to working on their limitations.

What is the work about? Employ constructive criticism that will help identify areas of improvement using a more well-rounded approach. Instead of simply criticizing the person, follow up the critique with a solution. Managers and leaders who offer solutions gain more respect and following if they back-up their criticism with relevant and valuable solutions.

Let us say an employee is constantly writing reports that are filled with grammatical errors. Rather than telling them that it is an issue and they shouldn't do it, explain the ramifications of the problem, followed by an actionable takeaway or solution. You can mention something such as "Though your research and content is fabulous, the grammatical mistakes are pointlessly ruining your reports." Or "If you work on your grammar and sentence construction, you'll create awesome reports." Set timelines and come up with a plan of action to help them work on their weaknesses. Simply telling someone to stop doing something doesn't make you an effective communicator.

This work in our personal life too! When you want someone to change something about them, offer them solutions and a plan of action. Mention the implications of continuing with it and how resolving/overcoming the limitation can better their lives. Honesty is important but it shouldn't border on being painfully blunt. Even though you aren't using the sandwich technique, you still have to keep it positive, polite, and encouraging if you want to get the other person to act on it.

Again, let us take the above example of an employee making too many grammatical errors in their reports. A personal attack in this scenario would be labeling them lazy, sloppy, careless, laidback, irresponsible, incapable, and so on. You are calling out the person instead of the main issue. Yes, they may be all of this. However, you won't get them to listen to you if you launch into a personal attack rampage.

Instead, call out the issue by installing faith in the person and letting them know that you believe "they are capable but just need to be more mindful while drafting their reports." Tell them that you know they are capable of fixing this issue and that it is no big deal for them. Let them know politely yet firmly that the issue needs to be addressed or rectified immediately because you want them to accomplish what you believe they are fully capable of accomplishing. Contrast this with calling out their laziness and inadequacy.

Personal attacks make people instinctively defensive. It shifts focus from the real problem and creates a psychological battle between two people who, more or less, want the same thing. The dynamics change when you make personal attacks, and it worsens the issue instead of rectifying it. Don't divert attention from the real issue by making the recipient of the feedback more defensive.

A person is less likely to be defensive about their actions if they are given an opportunity to rate their own performance.

Also, be specific in giving feedback. Compliments and criticism both should be specific. Avoid talking in vague and generalized terms. Instead, address a specific issue. Taking the above example, instead of telling the employee that their report was written "ineffectively" (which can imply anything from the writing style to research to grammatical errors to vocabulary), be specific and mention that "their grammar and sentence construction needs work in an otherwise put together report."

Being specific will help the other person identify the exact problem, thus, increasing your chances of getting him/her to take action in the right direction. While offering feedback, refer to specific instances and offer examples. For instance, if you are pulling up an employee for bad behavior, mention specific instances of his/her bad behavior.

Avoid acting on impulse or saying something you'll end up regretting later in a conflict-prone situation. Take time to think through your actions before responding. Mentally, go over the consequences of different actions instead of responding in a harsh and impulsive manner. If you think you need more clarification or a closer examination of facts, take time to seek it before responding. Instant reactions often border on the negative since our emotions are at the peak. Taking time off to analyze the situation more objectively gives us the opportunity to neutralize our emotions a bit.

Again, how to determine if conflict resolution should be kept private or enter the public arena? If the misunderstanding, miscommunication, or conflict happened in the private arena (mail, phone call, or person to person), restrict its resolution within the personal arena as well. However, if the conflict occurred in a public domain or publically, then deal with it publically. Irrespective of where it is brought out, aim to resolve the issues instead of letting it snowball into something bigger.

Build an opening for effective communication so everyone can express themselves or have their say. You can start by mentioning that there is a conflict or it has occurred. Later, add that everyone will be given an opportunity to have their say in the matter. Then, step back and allow people to have their say without any interruptions, judgmental statements, and emotional outbursts. Make it clear at the onset that everyone will be given an opportunity to air their views. This makes people open up, drop their guard, and feel heard.

Repeat your understanding of the issue. This is a part of active listening skills but deserves a special mention in conflict resolution. When there's a conflict, obviously, everyone perceives issues differently. Restate your understanding of the issue by saying something like "If I heard you correctly, I understand that you are not happy about the way things are shaping up with this project due to (reason for conflict)." It is important to make the other person feel heard. It not just confirms your understanding of the situation but also gives the other person an opportunity to correct you in case you've misinterpreted or misunderstood their words.

Use more "I" and less "You" statements during conflict resolution. By framing emotions, thoughts, and feelings around yourself, you accept responsibility for how you feel instead of blaming the other person. This prevents them from becoming defensive and adding to the conflict. "I' statements focus more on facts and resolution, while "you" statements are more emotionally laden. For instance, "You knew how important the client presentation was. Why were you still late for it?" Try framing the same by accepting responsibility for your own reactions. "I felt really upset and frustrated that we couldn't begin our client meeting on time." Now, instead of blaming the person, you are sticking to facts that led you to feel upset.

Let us look at some statements. Instead of saying, "Xyz never consults me or includes me in design-related decisions ever," try saying "I feel upset when I am unaware of the design-related decisions that affect my work until the decisions are already made" or "I find it tough to do the best work possible when I come to know about modifications needed after I've already given it a lot of time and effort." There can be a huge leap in your conflict resolution skills once you accept ownership of your feelings instead of focusing on other's faults and putting them in a defensive mode.

In the end, it is always a good practice to end a conflict by following up in an appropriate manner. Begin by restating the resolution after thanking the person for their involvement in resolving the issue and ensuring open communication. Tell them that you'll be around if they have any issues in the future. This helps to offer a logical closure to the conflict and ensures everyone accepts where you've all arrived.

Where conflicts are concerned (especially workplace conflicts), people often find someone to blame instead of going to the root cause of the matter. Focus on setting the process right instead of making this about a person or group of people. Ask yourself things such as "Did the person have all the relevant information to perform their task correctly? Was there an error in communication that led to the conflict? Was there contextual loss when information or knowledge shared hands?" Focusing on the issue allows you to prevent such conflicts from occurring in the future. It will also give people the confidence that you've got their back when things aren't hunky-dory, something that inspires greater faith and loyalty.

Receiving negative feedback effectively

Again, if you are on the other side of the feedback, avoid taking it personally. Understand that it doesn't speak about your capability or limitations as a person. Distance yourself from the issue or situation. Also, criticism or negative feedback isn't as bad as you think. It is only propelling your growth and taking you in the right direction. Depersonalize the criticism, and instead, focus on growth and development.

Instead, drop their guard by appealing to their rational or logical side. Admit you could be wrong, and that you want to be corrected if you are wrong. Then, go about examining the facts together to prove the other person wrong without making it obvious to them.

While responding to criticism, you can say something such as "I would really like to work on this and do everything I can to change it or find a way ahead." It will make you instantly endearing to the other person. Even something such as "Yes, I have noticed this issue myself. Can we work on a plan of action to help me overcome it?" You are accepting the issue instead of getting defensive. This immediately softens the other person's stand that will be likelier to work with a solution-oriented approach ahead.

Own up to your actions if you know you've goofed up. Accept accountability and responsibility for your actions instead of making excuses, which only ends up strengthening the other person's attacks. Owning your actions shows the other person that you are ready to work towards a solution. When you express thankfulness for the feedback, you are invariably leading yourself towards growth and development.

Avoid fighting facts. Our first instinctive reaction, when faced with facts, is to battle with reality and create our own version about our circumstances (which may be nothing but a bundle of excuses we give to rationalize our mistakes). We become helpless victims of situations and circumstances instead of accepting accountability for our actions. Reality is difficult to deal with, and more stress-causing. Offering excuses is the easier way out.

Instead, conserve your energy for understanding the valuable lesson held in the feedback. Respond in a manner that will help instead of hurt your future prospects. This will help in improving your overall performance. Rebuilding credibility comes easy when you take action in the required direction instead of justifying your mistakes. Instead of fighting glaring facts, accept them and move in the direction of improvement.

Push for lasting results. When faced with a setback, people often obstinately stick to their perception of reality. Stop digging your heels and justifying what you did! Don't be hell-bent on proving yourself right or the other person wrong. Ask yourself if you'd rather be proven right or embark on the path of growth and development. If you are right, you'll end up giving up valuable learning and amazing results. You'll give up on the opportunity to better yourself. You'll only seek misleading feedback that continues to reinforce that you are right instead of offering constructive criticism in the right direction. This way, you are blocking out solutions and information that can help you in the long run.

However, if you choose growth and development, you are moving in the direction of learning and becoming a better version of yourself. By accepting accountability, you transform from being a victim to a rational individual who is keen on focusing on change and development. This is the first step towards taking responsibility, learning lessons, gaining clarity on doing things differently, and finally, producing more effective results in the future. Accept negative feedback as helpful and valuable instead of hurtful to unlock all the positives that are in store for you.

Chapter 15: Tips and Tricks for Communication

The more you practice and the more skills you acquire the better off you will be when you actually find yourself in specific situations.

Body Language

When it comes to communication your body language plays a key role in bow you and your world are perceived. The first thing that you need to master is eye contact. When we talk to people if we can get them to look into our eyes we can begin to tell if they are lying, hiding something or are nervous. Eye contact is a key component in all communication.

Keeping your head raised up high. Another component in body language is how we h old up our heads. When we raise our heads up high and can look eye to eye with others it shows a level of confidence. When we have our heads hanging down low or we are moving our heads around looking at other tings in the room it is a tell sign that something isn't right.

Don't fidget with your fingers and hands. Another tell sign that you are not truthful or at least are nervous about a specific situation is how you deal with your hands. When we keep our hand still or when we are talking we move our hands we are showing emotion and confidence. If, however we are sitting still and we are tapping our fingers, biting our nails or just moving our hands up and down our clothing it shows others that we are not confident and are nervous.

There are many subtle signs when it comes to body language. When we take the time to learn all of these subtle movements and non-movements we can begin to build a picture of the internal conversations we are all having.

Participate in Conversation

Shy employees always think that their opinion won't be given importance and this fear does not let them speak up especially when they are asked to say something in a certain situation.

When you are asked to share your thoughts during the

meeting, you should not hesitate to do that, no matter how hard it seems to you, because it will be a crucial step towards building your confidence and breaking the shackles for you.

You must keep one thing in mind that others are giving value to your comments or suggestions, that's why they are asking you to speak.

Adjust Your Language According to whom You are Talking To

You wouldn't necessarily talk to your friends, family, co-workers, or acquaintances all in the same way. Effective communicators are the ones who are best able to tailor their messages to their targeted audience based on whom they are speaking to. So, whenever you are preparing to have a conversation with someone, remind yourself of whom you are talking to and get in the right frame of mind before having the discussion.

Be Concise and Specific

Practice being as concise as possible while still being able to include all the important and vital information that needs to be said or written. It may take a few practice sessions before you get the hang of it.

Being Positive

Imagine a situation where Person A is speaking in a bright, cheery manner with a smile on their face. Now, imagine Person B, who is speaking in sullen, somber tones with a serious look or frown on their face. Who would be most likely to capture your attention span? Person A of course. Always smile, because a positive attitude does make a difference, and nobody can resist a person who radiates with positive energy.

Be Mindful of Your Body Language

Effective communicators adopt an open, welcoming and inviting body language when they have a conversation with someone. Our bodies are capable of communicating without ever saying a word, so watch your body language when you are having a conversation if you want to be an effective communicator. Maintain good eye contact, never cross your arms in front of your body, smile, don't put your hands in your pockets, adopt a relaxed posture, and hold your head up high with confidence.

Keep Conversation Fillers Out

Conversation fillers here refer to the um's and the ah's that we don't even realize we are saying. Conversation fillers do nothing to help improve your communication skills. In fact, these fillers actually damper your efforts at becoming an effective communicator because too many um's and ah's makes it seem like you are unsure of yourself and what you want to say.

Say No to Distractions

Nobody likes being interrupted every few minutes when they're trying to have an important discussion. That happens all too often, especially today when mobile phones have dominated our everyday existence. To be an effective communicator, you are going to need to make an effort to put away all the distractions before you carry out a conversation, no matter who it is you may be speaking to. If you are talking to someone, they deserve your full and undivided attention. So, put the mobile phones and gadgets away and for those few minutes, just focus on the person you are talking to.

Avoid Talking Over the Person

Being a good communicator means demonstrating mutual respect for the person you are talking to. When it is their turn to communicate with you, don't interrupt them or talk over them in a louder voice that you end up drowning out their opinion. Talking over the person makes them feel disgruntled, and they will be less receptive to what you have to say in turn, so your effective communication efforts will be gone to waste.

Communicate with Patience

Everyone is different and processes information differently. Not everyone will be able to receive the information in the same manner or timeliness that you might. When communicating with other people, you need to keep that in mind and be patient in your explanation and descriptions. If they need more clarification, give it to them. Do everything that you can to make clear what it is you are trying to say. It is easy to get impatient with someone when they find it difficult to grasp immediately information that seems easy to you, but remind yourself once again that not everyone has the same level of communication. Demonstrating patience in your communication will also make the other person feel comfortable enough to ask more questions and be more receptive to what you have to say.

Prepare for Presentation

You don't have to panic whenever it's your turn to do the presentation but you should focus on things that motivate you to do it in a successful way. Tell yourself that you have to avail every opportunity that comes in your way and you have to prove your professional abilities and skills to show your superiors that you can be an asset for the organization.

Keep practicing until you feel comfortable doing it because practice is the only thing that can bring perfection in any skill.

You can also record yourself with a video camera and watch that video to judge yourself from others perspective, this way you will be able to find your weak points and work on them.

You can analyze that what standing posture will suit you the best and overall how your body language is supposed to be, so that you look impressive while doing the presentation and everybody pays attention to what you say.

Don't Be Afraid of Fumbles

When you are in the process of improving your communication skills, you are most likely to have fumbles while you are talking at one point or the other. You don't have to be affected by this, keeping in mind throughout the conversation what happened. Just put that thing off your mind, and focus on what you are saying currently.

It's obvious that you will want to learn from your mistakes, so next time you do things in a better way without repeating them, and this is what your mind is supposed to be focused on all the time.

Listen to Your Seniors

You will start noticing a big change in your confidence and ability to communicate with excellence in any situation when you start spending more time among those colleagues whose experience can benefit you.

You can listen what they have got to share as the more you interact with them, the more you will learn from them which ultimately results in the development of your better communication skills.

Listen to the senior colleagues as much as you can because you have to be a great listener first of all, and the better you listen, the better you speak. This strategy will definitely make you successful in giving your opinion in a pompous way.

Set Small Targets

It's a great idea to monitor your progress by yourself on daily basis. You can set small targets for every day, and see whether you achieve them or not at the end of the day.

Never be aggressive or defensive

This goes back to the point of keeping our emotions in check. When we speak we tend to dig deep down into our emotional selves. When we draw from our emotions we tend to speak first rather than sit back and think of the words that come out of our mouths. This form of communication will end up causing you more problems than they are worth. Another reason you don't want to be aggressive or defensive is that when we are calm and collected we tend to get our points across better than if we were to be combative. If you were to be in a conversation where every idea or statement that you made was challenged or told was wrong how would you react?

When we act in this fashion we will never elicit change. In fact, when we act this way people will not want to include us in the decision making process and more than likely make decisions on their own. So, when it comes to aggression and defensive attitudes you want to keep them in check. They will do more harm than good.

Don't deviate

Another thing that you will want to do when communicating with others is stay the course and don't deviate from your original thoughts. This is a huge issue when trying to get your point across to some people.

When you have a specific issue that you want to talk

about you don't want to jump all around the board. For example, if you are stating that you are pro in the conversation you don't want to start making comments that are negative or go against your initial points.

When we don't deviate and are confident in our initial statements people will take our words more seriously. If, however we jump around and talk about a million different things then people will get confused and our initial meaning as well as our own train of thought will become muddled.

Be confident in your ideas

Another thing that you will want to do is make sure that you have confidence in your ideas and the points that you want to communicate. When we have an idea such as how to make a product better or how to get more customers into the store we need to make sure that we are confident in this train of thought.

Once this statement is made people will begin to process what it is that you have said and begin to form questions that will be either for that idea, against the idea or both. If you make this statement and end up having no concept on how to implement it or ways to improve upon it then people will look at you clueless and looking for some form of direction to make your idea a reality. If however you can support your idea then you will have a better chance to making it a reality instead of someone else taking over the concept and turning the idea into their own.

Use the correct communication method

When communicating with others it is your job to learn the best way the person you are talking to can process information. In many cases we only rely on verbal communications. This is typically the best way to communicate but it isn't the only way to communicate. In many situations communication through visual ques such as pictures, graphs, video and even audio will help illustrate your point and will in the long run allow people to process this information in their own way.

When we take the time to use other forms of communication we increase the likelihood that others will understand what it is we are saying and in turn can also give feedback and pointers to improving our thoughts.

End conversations with a hardy handshake

The handshake is the universal greeting and farewell that people use when starting and ending conversations. When we enter a room or meet someone for the first time we typically extend our hand out and grasp the other person's hand firmly. This sets a physical connection between the two parties. From here eye contact is engaged increasing the personal connection between the two people.

When engaging in a handshake a set amount of pressure is exerted on the hands. This is a tell sign between the two people and sometimes set the tone for dominance. For instance, if one hand exerts more pressure than the others the one with the most pressure is considered to be the more dominant person. Depending on the mental state of the individuals involved this could set the entire tone for the conversation as well as the tone for the overall relationship.

Write down everything

One of the best ways to learn to communicate as well as other tings is life is to write them down. One thing that you can do when writing things down is to write short stories. These short stories will put you in control of the actions and inactions of others.

For example, if you start with two characters in a room. In this room they have a box that needs to be opened. What you can do is start out by writing the conversation that each person would have. You can then jump into writing about the inner dialogue that each person is having. You can talk about what they are thinking compared to what they actually say. You can talk about their body language, their fears, hopes and desires.

At the end of the story you can conclude it with different endings. For example, could the box be a birthday or Christmas present. Who give the present to this individual and what is their relationship status? When we write down these stories we can begin to train our brains to react and even anticipate actions and events that may occur in real life. If you are having trouble coming up with a story or a plot just go back to a time in your life where you had a conversation with someone that didn't go well. Start writing down what happened exactly how it occurred in real life and then make marks in the story where you wish you had made a different decision or choice. From there you can flesh out the story and make it your own. Then the next time you find yourself in this situation or a similar situation you can craft the real life story to reach your intended outcome.

Chapter 16: How to Develop Good Communication Skills?

In order to develop healthy communication skills, it is crucial that you become ready to completely shed off your old skin and turn into a new person altogether. Sticking to your old self won't help since communication requires you to open up and spread out as much as possible.

Everyone hears, very few listen. The first step to a good communication is listening. It's only when you hear the other party that you grasp how to respond. Blabber on your own track and you fail to be a communicator from the very start.

Speak

Ever since man's stopped using sign language to communicate, speaking has dominated his usage of tongue to convey information. What would you call speaking? Using words to send relevant data? Speaking has evolved into more than a mere sending of words.

Speaking is the use of tongue to convey emotions, intentions and information to other people. It helps you make others understand what you want, know or feel. If it were not for speaking, humans would have still used hand gestures to show they are hungry, sleepy or horny. Just imagine such a scenario.

Speaking opens not only your mouth but also your mind. The action of speaking requires and pushes you to think. Thinking is an activity that keeps you engaged mentally. When you think, you naturally develop and sharpen your mind. Your mind opens shut doors to let you think and speak. You start accepting new ways to form opinions and to put them out for others to see.

There is no limit to your wings of imagination. You start exploring new dimensions and seeing better ways to perceive people. Basically, you change your personality in such a manner that others notice changes in you. Speaking therefore, opens you up. It removes fetters from your development and lets you witness the best you can achieve. Speaking is an art, which when mastered, covers almost more than half of your communication skills.

Mind your body language

Body language could be defined as a combination of all those physical activities that you unintentionally perform that depicts your intentions and emotions. The amount of communication you perform by your body language is almost as equivalent as the amount you perform by what you say.

Communication isn't always vocal. It assumes different forms like eye movements, talking style, hand gestures and general hand movements. Body language is a good way to avoid using words and ensuring quick sending of messages. It's easy and smart to communicate without putting any special efforts into it. Talking is good, sure, but what if you had better options to convey information? Body language is the answer.

Spice up

Everyone speaks. But those who leave an impression behind on their listeners' minds are the ones remembered. Simply constructed sentences and casually picked up words hardly do justice to a speaker's image. When you do not infuse life into your words, you fail to impress those listening. By life, I mean excitement, appeal and class. When you make your conversations funny, witty and sarcastic, you open new doors of possibilities.

So how do you go about spicing up your conversations? If there's a possibility for a fun angle being added to your sentences, go for it. Do not hesitate to imagine well and imbibe the said imagination into your words. Cleverly selected words have more magic than casually said ones.

Briefness is another character that elevates your conversation's worth. The briefer your sentences, more the impact you leave behind. A study found that shorter sentences have more conviction powers than longer ones. When you wrap up your conversations with short sentences, you allow the other party to think back-something that is not possible with long sentences. When you allow the listeners to think upon what you have just said, they realize it makes sense.

On the contrary, when you do not allow such time, they assume you are either bluffing or trying to dominate the proceedings. Shorter sentences therefore, enhance your impact as a communicator.

Sarcasm is a trait not everyone possesses. It is the rare quality to whiplash someone without them knowing that you have just owned them. The quality of sarcasm is a funny way to get back to those opposite you. If you master the quality well, you could enter into any argument blind-folded. Though seen as a last resort in a debate, it serves a great deal when you want to make the opposite party regret locking horns with you. Being a good communicator requires the inculcation of the characteristic of sarcasm in your skills-set.

Another quality that needs to be possessed by you in order for you to turn into a good communicator is humor. Humor never fails to entertain listeners. If you have this trait on your side, you not only end up making your point but also make the audience laugh.

The purpose of conveying through a message is accompanied by the incentive of a funny laugh. However, when you communicate you should guard against excessive or negative humor. Humor in excess dilutes the conversation and shifts the direction from your conversation to fun. The very purpose of having a conversation is defeated. Negative humor is that which offends race, gender, and similar sensitive issues. Refrain from using negative humor in your communication as it will show you in a bad light.

A good conversation involves both the parties to it- the speaker and the listener. Both the parties are accorded equal importance and neither predominates over the other. If this balance is disturbed, a conversation steers away from its purpose. Such a balance is mandatory for any conversation to achieve an ideal stage from whence it receives not only acknowledgement but also applause from the audience.

When an already perfect conversation is infused with things like fun, sarcasm, witticism and intellect, the impact such a conversation has on its listeners is huge. A bland and dry conversation is only informative. But a conversation that is infused with the mentioned traits does more than informing. It keeps the parties excited and informed. It makes them crave for more and never bores them throughout the conversation. The communication you perform this way is an ideal one.

Read

Reading is a habit that when inculcated in a human reaps him numerous benefits. When you read, you explore the world. New doors of shining experiences get open and you start seeing things through other people's perspectives. You get yourself familiar with people, their views and their angle of thinking. Reading familiarizes you with images that you never thought would be possible.

The habit of reading is vital to be infused at a young age. When children are taught to not just learn reading but also keep continuing it, they have a particular thing to return to. With age, this habit turns into a hobby and kids start exploring various genres. Be it fiction or autobiographies, they cannot keep their hands off books in general. They squeal upon coming across a bookshop and spend all their pocket money on buying books. The art of buying second-hand is more pronounced in your kids than it may be in you. Tender minds are like clean slates. Whatever you write on them will stay for a long time in their lives. When you introduce kids to such a healthy habit, you essentially push them towards being a good communicator.

Socialize

When you meet new people, you pick up their stories and experiences. Everyone has learnt a lot of lessons from their lives. When they share it with others, they allow them to become a part of their stories. By becoming a part of their stories, you learn the lessons they learnt. The very essence of communication is that it is to be facilitated by at least one party. When you are the one doing it, you need to pick up the social courage to do it. If you shy away from social company, you are killing any chances of socializing, and hence by extension, communication.

Socialization is the art of mingling with the society. It requires you to gel well with those who are not a part of your family. You may know your family members very well but that's not the case with others.

Upon socializing, you choose to allow others the chance to know you and get familiar with your experiences. Such discretion in social gathering opens your dam-gates of mind. You no longer shut yourself down in your room getting busy with online social networking. You start attending social gatherings and mingle with other members of the society. Those who didn't know you before start getting familiar with you. Socialization is a necessary performance to be performed by anyone who wishes to develop his communication skills.

The very act of communication requires that there has to be one audience. Who better a candidate than society? The little talks you have in a kitty party, the jokes you enjoy sharing in your club's meetings, the interesting people you meet in your tennis club; it all helps your communication skills in this way or other.

Society is the base of communication. If communication were bacteria, society would be its petri-dish where it's cultivated and grown for further spreading. If it were not for the society, communication would have developed as a skill. It is only when we start mingling with others that the art of communication gets pronounced.

Keep improving your vocabulary

It is a common experience that we do not find the right words for the right things. This happens because of a neglected or unimproved vocabulary. Vocabulary is the human storehouse of words that one uses while expressing himself orally.

This oral mishap happens because we either haven't been practicing on our vocabulary or it's been that redundant since the start. Vocabulary is a like a pet; you just don't stop at buying a dog; you have to get it vaccinations, feed it pedigree and look after its bath schedules from time to time. You might also have to train him to poop at the right place!

Your vocabulary is nothing very different from a pet dog. You have to train your vocabulary from time to time in order to make sure it's functioning smoothly.

To ensure kits efficiency you must keep adding words to it. Not just addition, deletion is important too. There are always words that get scrapped or out of usage with time. Keep modifying your vocabulary to meet your situations.

Always have a dictionary at hand. These days, you also have an option for downloading an online dictionary that can be accessed even when you are offline. There are many applications for smart phones that teach you one word a day.

A good vocabulary is that one which always has backups stored. A word has not only synonyms but also antonyms. Get yourself familiar with all the synonyms and antonyms of a new word that you learn. It also helps to know the origin of the word, but it's not mandatory. Apart from having backed up words, it's really worth it to know the minute difference between two similar sounding words. Here's a little example to explain this:

There are two words that sound strikingly similar and are yet brilliantly different from each other. 'Alone' and 'Lonely' are often used interchangeably by people who do not pay much attention to the intricacies of their vocabulary. However, a real communicator who knows better than to mix up his words would know the real difference.

The word 'alone' is used in situations where you need to describe physical isolation. When a person is only physically single, he's alone. But the word 'lonely' is used to talk about situations that describe a person who is only mentally single. When you feel lonely, you are likely to be sad. But when you are alone, you are only single in terms of physical company. Sadness is more likely to happen in the latter case.

A good communicator always knows the exact difference between two similar sounding words. This saves you from social embarrassment.

Vocabulary used to have a very narrow definition attached to it. The old description had the meaning of vocabulary to imply something that consisted of only words. However, a more liberal form of definition says that an ideal vocabulary is more about than just words. A healthy vocabulary should always include things like idioms, wit and other necessary literary devices.

Communication skills require the application of not

just your word knowledge but also the optimum accompanied action. The tone with which you speak, the manner which you adopt while speaking and the kind of impression your words leave behind; they all add up to develop a good vocabulary.

Chapter 17: How to Be a Charismatic Conversationalist and Increase Your Social Charisma

How can you build an irresistible social persona or magnetic social power? What are the traits that differentiate ace communicators from regular ones? What are the unspoken, hidden x-factors that reality show judges look for in contestants?

Make others feel special

Some of the world's most powerful communicators understand the importance of making other people feel special. They earn a loyal following based on their ability to make others feel valued, cherished and great about themselves. Charismatic communicators know how to hold a compelling conversation by concentrating on other people's life, passions, and interests. They demonstrate a genuine interest in people. People seldom forget how you make them feel even if they don't remember what you did or didn't do for them. Use this to your benefit through every given opportunity to make people feel special about them! Speak about their strengths, encourage/hail them publicly, and highlight their positives – basically, place them on a pedestal to increase your own likeability and charisma.

Express discomfort or have tough conversations with ease

At times, we have no choice but to have difficult, uncomfortable conversations with people or communicate with difficult people. The manner in which you handle these potentially conflict-laden and tricky situations contribute to our overall popularity. You don't need to go guns and daggers after people if you disagree with them. There can be disagreements and conflicts between people all the time in personal, professional and social settings. However, prevent them from snowballing into something bigger.

When you have something uncomfortable to say to the other person or discuss it with them, say something like, "Jill, I need to speak to you about something that has been troubling me for long. This way you are assuming responsibility for experiencing a particular feeling rather than accusing the other person. When you begin your sentence in the manner mentioned above, the other person immediately lowers his/her defenses and becomes more open and receptive to what you are saying.

Adapt to multiple communication styles

This is as important for leaders as for people seeking more harmonious interpersonal relationships. Adapting to different communication styles in integral to the process of a being an effective communicator and speaker.

Likewise, when you are communicating with baby boomers, you'll use a different communication approach than if you are communicating with Millennials. While baby boomers are more open to personal, face to face communications, Millennials may prefer emails, instant messaging and video conferencing.

As a leader or communicator, you'll be required to tune in to the preferences, personalities, demographics and communication style of your team members or audience. Even in personal encounters, you may have to adapt to your partner's or friend's communication style to build more harmonious and fulfilling relationships.

Be a smart observer

Some of the best conversationalists and most effective communicators I know are the ones who notice and talk details. Ever wondered by fiction authors and professional scriptwriters weave such wonderfully imaginative stories, concepts, and ideas? Artists, poets, writers and other creative professionals are brilliant observers. They skillfully notice things and people around them to create ideas, images, and characters. They are pros at observing and absorbing diverse situations while giving it their own interpretation. These are the people who will offer detailed compliments or comment on a fascinating wall artifact or jewelry piece someone's wearing at a party. They will quickly notice people's accents and start talking to them about it. Their conversations are based on detailed and interesting observations. It comes with practice. Start being more observant and conscious of people and things around you! Give yourself a clear conversation edge by noticing small details that a majority of people overlook. You will come across as an exciting, creative and interesting conversationalist who is in sync with the listener.

Offer interesting, detailed an exciting insight into your conversation. Avoid speaking or talking regarding expected, basic or simplistic. Don't state the obvious. Instead of talking about the latest breaking news that people must've heard a hundred times by now, offer your own unique take or view of it to make the interaction more memorable. Keep some trivia handy or know interesting/fun facts at the back of your hand, and pepper your conversation with it. I also like reading about interesting research in the field of human behavior and psychology, which is almost always a winner. People enjoy talking about psychological research, self-help topics, and behavioral patterns. Pop psychological insights also make for an interesting conversation topic, which appeals to a majority of people.

Always offer one or two useful takeaways

Offer people something to take back irrespective of whether you are addressing a single person or a group of people who are struggling with an issue. Always end your talk or conversation with a couple of actionable, practical and realistic takeaways can be applied in their daily life. It will increase the value of your conversations, and make interacting with you more desirable.

Avoid talking to people in a patronizing or sermonizing manner when they share an issue or problem with you. I know plenty of people who talk down to others or imply that they've been really foolish to get into xyz situation. Don't do that. Talking down to people never helps. You'll seldom win people by making them feel miserable about themselves. Instead, empathize with them, and offer practical solutions. Unsolicited opinions and sermons serve no purpose. Give them an actionable piece of advice they can start implementing immediately. At the end of the conversation, they should have a valuable and doable solution.

Employ the power of personal stories

Charismatic communicators know how to make themselves irresistible, likable and relatable by narrating personal experiences and anecdotes. They make their interactions even more interesting, fascinating and personal by sharing their own stories as examples or to demonstrate to the other person how they've been in a similar situation. It makes them come across as more identifiable and relatable. This technique also helps create a common foundation for establishing deeper and more meaningful relationships with people.

Confidence is the key factor

Confidence and self-assuredness don't equal arrogance. It is being comfortable in your skin and having faith in your capabilities. Keep a polite, well-mannered, courteous and assertive stance while communicating with people.

Develop the art of speaking with conviction. If you want to develop greater confidence, stand in the front of the mirror while talking. This helps you realize how you come across to others while talking. You'll also identify areas of improvement to boost overall confidence.

Confidence is a huge component of charisma. Also, it is an evolving trait. It's a work in progress. If something is destroying your confidence or making you feel inadequate about yourself, pin it down. There can be some things from speech to hair to knowledge. Focus on growing your positives, and improving your weaknesses. Boost your personal appearance, skills, posture, and knowledge to make you feel wonderful about yourself.

Use humor to your advantage

Ask the next 10-20 people you interact with what makes a person highly irresistible to them, and a majority will most likely respond with a fabulous sense of humor. Who doesn't like people who make them laugh! People with a wonderful sense of humor are attractive, popular and much sought after everywhere. They have people hooked to everything they say and do. There is an unmistakable charisma surrounding them. Ever thought about why Oprah Winfrey is among the wealthiest and most sought-after television/media personalities? She is a wonderful blend of humor, honesty, and empathy (one of the most killer combinations when it comes to winning people).

Make other people laugh, and activate their feel-good hormones. You will always have a solid edge over others if you can make people smile or laugh. Have you observed how you are likely to buy from salespeople who make you laugh? Contrast this with people who simply go on and on about a product's features in a tiring monotone. We all know how men/women with a totally dig-worthy sense of humor have the most attractive girls/boys flocking to them. They are the subject of absolute envy. Start developing a sense of humor today by reading more, watching funny content, and coming up with your own creative lines (think about the most hilarious thing you can say in any situation).

Be genuine and authentic

This should be understood, but it's funny how many get it completely wrong. They put on pretenses, and come across as highly obnoxious and preposterous to others. Do not pretend to be something you clearly aren't.

While it alright to fake a little confidence to be able to be practice being more at ease in social relationships and develop greater self-assuredness in social situations, don't try to project something you are not just to be popular. Once the mask wears off, people will discover the truth and stay miles away from you. Make a conscious to increase your charisma, become more influential and develop a more persuasive communication style, while still being true to yourself. Stay natural, authentic and trustworthy. You should come across genuine to other people to inspire their trust and increase your likeability factor.

Chapter 18: Techniques to Master Every Communication

Here are 10 communication techniques to master, each is just as important in personal and social life, as well as at work or outside the office with your colleagues. By learning these techniques by heart, you will be able to quickly connect to anyone, earn their respect, and gain influence.

Be Friendly.

People are drawn to signs of friendliness. People with a smiling face and pleasing personality always have an edge in every communication. Friendly people bring an automatic wave of calmness; they put people at ease, enabling them to open up and speak freely. This is a must, especially when your aim is to practice your communication skills. People who are ready to listen and share will make everything easier for any speaker.

Never sound like a fool.

Think before you speak. Be prudent enough to think first before talking about something. People who never filter their words are often considered reckless. It is important to always know what you are talking about. And even if you know what you are talking about, make sure that you are sensitive enough to tell if what you are saying will produce a negative reaction among your listeners. People with good communication skills often leave their listeners inspired and feeling great.

Clear as crystal.

If you want to excel in communication, find ways to convey your message in a brief and clear manner. Avoid being indirect as it would only confuse your listeners. You would not want to leave your audience bewildered and asking what it was you really meant.

Too much is always bad.

Be concise, less is always good when conveying your message. Never attempt to sound "intellectual" by injecting too many words. Also, never use jargons and difficult words just to project an impressive image. No matter how many words you use, how many sentences, if your listeners are not able to absorb what you are saying, then you fail as a speaker.

Be Authentic.

Integrity, humility, and honesty are very important when conveying something. People have the natural ability to detect inconsistencies in what others are saying, so never pretend just to win over your listeners.

Be confident.

Humility is never about the lack of confidence. On the other hand, humility is about knowing what you are capable of and knowing your limitations. The self-awareness you get from humility should be enough to boost your confidence. Speak with a conviction that you know what you are saying; use appropriate tone to convince them of your honesty and sincerity. Make eye contact to draw them to you and the things you want to say to them.

Body language.

Hand gestures and facial expressions will always make it easier for your listeners to understand what you are saying. So, use them to your advantage and eliminate the chances of being misunderstood. Your body language will put real meaning to the words you are using.

Tone is everything.

Whether you are face to face with someone or you are speaking to somebody over the phone, your tone plays a big part in perfecting your communication skills. Words are naked without the proper tone. Tone gives your words the authority they need to be absorbed by your listeners. Over the phone, tone dresses you up in the mind of the listener.

Positive scripting.

Words are powerful. With the right vocabulary and the right tone, you can make other people feel better. Practice using positive words in conveying your thoughts and emotions even when telling something about a challenging experience. In doing so, people around you will always feel happy when with you.

Listen.

It is only natural to be drawn to someone who is a great listener. Even when you are not connecting with anyone, people will remember you if you take this technique by heart, they may even contact you when they need to talk to someone. It will be a huge compliment on your part when someone contacts you and invite you for a quick chat. This shall be a clear sign that you are moving forward in your quest to acquire good communication skills.

Follow these techniques and you will never go wrong. When your listeners are able to feel good when talking to you, they will open up to you more and share. In return, they themselves can make your job as the speaker a lot easier. The aim of the techniques above is to make sure that you always establish a good rapport with your listeners. With enough practice, you will find out that your very positive presence is enough to draw people around you.

Chapter 19: Applying communication skills when Communicating with Strangers

However much you detest it, meeting and interacting with strangers is an integral and inescapable part of your life. We come across people we know nothing about in our everyday life. The good news is there are some smart tricks on hand to get strangers to like you immediately.

Use Their Name Multiple Times

Strangers don't really expect you to use their names as soon as they introduce themselves to you or are introduced to you by a third person. Plus, people are naturally wired to adore the sweet sound of their names (narcissism pays). Once you get to know someone's name, use it a few times during the conversation naturally.

Don't overdo it or it'll come across as fake. I always

notice when I address customer service representatives with their names a few times during the call, they become even more eager to help. The person invariably feels a sense of connection or friendliness towards you. The icy vibes of being strangers thaw a bit and he/she becomes more familiar when they address you by your name.

Also, when you repeat a person's name more than once, the chances of remembering it increase. This can save you the embarrassment of forgetting names (and permanently burying your chances of being liked by the person).

Smile and Maintain Eye Contact

This one's a no-brainer all the way. Smiling a universal expression of linking or opening up to someone. Offer strangers a genuine and warm smile to increase feelings of familiarity. It makes you come across as more approachable, amicable and friendly. Plus, it establishes a more positive tone for future interactions. The tiny act of smiling leads the brain into releasing chemical hormones that make you feel happier as a person. This way, you'll enter into an interaction feeling friendlier, happier and more positive, which invariably makes you more likable.

Eye contact is a universal expression or signals of confidence, transparency, honesty, and genuineness. More than 50 percent of our communication happens visually.

Use the Head Tilt

The head tilt is a wonderful non-verbal way to communicate your interest to a stranger or to get a stranger to like you. This communicates subconsciously to the other person that you aren't a threat to them because you are exposing your carotid artery. It is the primary artery that supplies blood to your brain, and any damage to this artery can lead to instant death or permanent brain damage. By exposing this region of your body, you are signaling to the stranger that neither are they a threat to you nor are you a threat to them. You are non-verbally setting the stage for a non-threatening relationship.

Use Empathetic Statements

Empathetic statements help retain the focus on another person, thus making you come across as more likable. People generally like the focus to be on themselves and not others. They feel wonderful when they are the center of attention. Don't parrot their statements for it may come across as patronizing or condescending. Rephrase what they've said while keeping the focus on them. The standard formula for creating empathetic statements should be, "So, what you are feeling or saying is….."

This immediately makes them the focus of the conversation. Something like, "I understand how you are feeling." The idea is to always have the other person as the focus of your conversation. This basic formula seldom goes wrong when it comes to being liked by strangers.

Ask for Favors

I know this seems amusing and even counterintuitive. I mean if you asked someone for a favor and they did fulfill it, you'd like them, right? However, Ben Franklin noticed that each time he asked co-workers for a favor, they liked him more than when he didn't ask for favors. This can work for strangers too when it comes to breaking the ice and opening up people towards you. "Oh you work for XYZ Company; I was really hoping to get the contact details of the marketing manager for a brand association or tie-up. I'd be really nice if you could help me with their contact details."

When someone does a favor, they feel great about themselves, and if you ask a person for a favor you are helping them feel wonderful about themselves. This goes a long way toward increasing your likeability quotient. It makes the person who is doing the favor bigger or focus of attention, which makes them feel good. However, don't overdo when it comes to asking people favors just so they like you more. Asking for too many favors will have people running in the opposite direction.

Talk to Strangers All the Time

If you'd given me this piece of advice a few years ago, I'd freak out. I mean I can go around stranger hopping, having happy conversations with strangers. I mean this goes against everything we've been taught since childhood about staying away from strangers.

Don't be bothered too much about making a glowing first impression. They are trying to make you like them as much you are trying to get them to like you, so it is an even game. Don't overthink or over-strategize how to approach people. Just be natural, friendly and approachable. Focus on everything that can be controlled, including the direction of the conversation.

Keep Your Body Language Open and Approachable

Did you know that strangers form an impression about you within the first four seconds of seeing or meeting you? The first four seconds are highly crucial when it comes to forming an impression about unknown people. This means the person will form an opinion about you even before you probably say anything at all! The onus in such cases is on your non-verbal signals or body language. Keep your body language relaxed and open.

Of course, actions speak louder than words. They work on a very subconscious and primordial level. Keep your gestures, posture, expressions, leg movements etc. more approachable. This can help determine on a subconscious level whether strangers view you as an open and receptive person. Your body language will determine whether a person likes you or not, irrespective of what you say.

Keep your palms and arms open if you want to come across as a more approachable and receptive person.

This makes you more likable to strangers because you come across as someone who is high on energy, expression, and enthusiasm. You come across as a more expressive, animated and articulate person. People respond more positively to people who are animated in their gestures.

Offer Sincere and Specific Compliments

Instead of telling someone how wonderful their outfit is, you can say the cut looks superb on them or you love the way the fit of the attire. Similarly, instead of telling someone that he/she is a good speaker, pick out bits and pieces from the conversation that you really enjoyed. Another favorite is, instead of saying, "you are beautiful" or "you have lovely eyes" say something like, "The color of your eyes is beautiful" or "you have a very soulful pair of eyes." Start with a warm smile, maintain eye contact, and then compliment them on their eyes. It works wonders!

Applaud them for the humor they used in the speech or their powerful vocabulary. Making the compliment specific makes you come across as more genuine than a plain flattery person. Compliments are a great way to get into the good books of strangers.

Make People Laugh

For all the communication tips I give people, this one probably tops the list when it comes to breaking the ice with strangers. People will adore you if you make them laugh. It is no secret that salespersons who make their potential customers laugh score high sales figures or customer service representatives who make customers laugh score high on customer satisfaction.

Ensure that you don't crack offensive jokes or resort to humor related to sensitive issues such as religion, race etc. Keep it clean, intelligent, simple and healthy. People are generally stressed, exhausted, and bored with their daily grind. When you resort to humor, you lighten up their day by making them laugh. It gives them a break from a mundane existence which makes you endearing to them. If they tell you they are having a tough day or were late for work today, give it a more light-hearted-spin. This will transform their sullen mood and make them more receptive to a conversation.

Chapter 20: How to Communicate with People to Build Friendships

Friendship, however, is incredibly important. Friends help relieve stress, make you happier, give advice, and just generally make your life better. How do you make lasting friendships like that?

Choose Carefully

You cannot be friends with everyone. Well, maybe you could, but it is not recommended. It is best to remain acquaintances with people until you have time to 'test the waters' and see how you feel about the other person. If you feel awkward or out of place, this is probably not the person you are looking for. If you are relaxed and feel as though you are able to be yourself around this person and speak easily, then you have found a good candidate.

Honesty

The key to any relationship is to be honest and genuine. The same goes for friendship. You can't be good friends with fake people. Don't be afraid to open yourself up. Always speak the truth and be authentically yourself. When you share stories, allow your new friends to see the emotions the story causes, lay yourself out there. Does this open you up for heartache and hurt? Yes, in a way, but it also lays down a foundation of trust and compassion decent people will not be able to deny. Give your friend compliments, it is totally okay. Also, be thankful when they give you compliments, but remember to be humble and stay grounded.

Don't Be Afraid of Silence

When speaking of communication, people assume that means you have to actually speak. This is not so. We have all heard or experienced the so-called awkward silence. The beauty of a true friendship is that there is no awkwardness in the silence. You are able to sit together and just do things quietly without feeling like you should get up and go. This kind of silence speaks volumes about trust and mutual respect.

Don't Step Down

If for some reason you and your friend find yourselves at odds, do not back down. Never walk away from an argument. Take the time to calmly make your side known, careful to keep your tone level and your words small. Make clear what the problem is and how you feel about it. Then, be sure to offer your friend the same in return. Be an active listener, look them in the eye, use your body language to show that you are interested in the conversation, and do not interrupt.

Communication is a useful tool in more professional relationships as well. You can use these skills to market and network yourself to the general public in order to boost your business and get your name out.

Chapter 21: Make your Conversations Unique and Memorable

We hold so many conversations in our daily lives with family, colleagues, business associates, acquaintances, bosses, neighbors, and even strangers. Most of them are soon forgotten; then there are those that linger in our minds for a long time. What separates the common conversation from truly great ones? Here's how to have unique conversations:

Full concentration

We often hold conversations when also concentrating on something else; a task, TV or phone. Multitasking has become a standard operating procedure. By the end of the conversation, neither party can outline what was said in the conversation. Make your conversation unique by paying full attention. Maintain a steady 70 – 80% eye contact. It will be a refreshing change for people that are used to being listened to just partially. If you're a fan of meditation, we call this listening mindfully. Mindfulness basically refers to living at the moment and enjoying all aspects of it. When you listen mindfully, you're attentive to every detail. The speaker will feel valued, appreciated and cared for, and will have no problem opening up.

Compliments

Throw in a genuine kind word here and there. It helps break the ice and places the discussion on a positive stand. As the conversations go on, you can identify more areas that deserve a compliment. Let's say people are talking about their careers. Somebody in the group mentions that they work for a particular real estate company. You happen to know that (remember what we said about staying informed?) that company is undertaking a massive project in the neighboring county. You can congratulate the speaker on the work 'they' are doing. Let the compliments be brief; just a sentence or two. The effect is still outstanding. The receiver feels noticed, appreciated and validated. With such a lifted spirit, the conversation is bound to be remembered for a long time.

Balance speaking and listening

This is a balance that is so often lacking, yet even those responsible for it could be doing so subconsciously. There are those self-absorbed people that will go on a monologue while everybody else is quiet. Such a scenario may even be thought of as a positive thing; 'they're all letting me speak since I'm the expert.' Unless you're giving a speech to an audience, dominating the dialogue as such is inappropriate. You risk coming across as proud and arrogant. However well you know the subject matter, or how good your oratory skills are, give the others an opportunity to speak.

You may be on the other side of the coin, where you hardly say anything in conversations. You're the quiet listener. Anything wrong with this approach? Absolutely. A conversation is a team effort. Whether you're engaging one other person or a group of people, all parties should participate. When you remain silent, the interlocutor(s) are inwardly trying to figure out why. Is the conversation boring? Are you not interested in the topic of discussion? Or are you devoid or content to contribute? See? You're taking their mental energy away from the conversation and tasking them with the burden of trying to interpret your actions. All this can be avoided if you contribute periodically, and facilitate a truly memorable conversation.

Steer the conversation

Once you break the ice with small talk, don't dwell there for long. Small-talk is unfulfilling and gets people easily bored. Pick cues of the interlocutor's interests from the conversation. From there, direct the conversation towards a deeper issue. From casual comments about the speakers in a conference, you can ask a question like, 'what do you expect the presenters will address this afternoon?' You can then talk about your expectations for the meeting and other relevant matters concerning the event.

Similarly, a random comment about sleeping in for the weekend can be turned into a more meaningful conversation about rest, unwinding, working hard vs working smart, work-related stress and so on. A deep conversation makes a lasting impression.

Use technology

We have stated before that you should avoid your gadgets when having a conversation, but isn't there an exception to every rule? If you've tried all means and the conversation still ends up stalling, you can compromise a bit. Refer to something interesting, informative, funny or relevant that you can come across online. Say something like; 'have you watched this documentary on the long-term effects of these Chinese loans?' Go ahead and steam the clip from your phone or laptop. It does not have to belong. And if it is, you don't have to watch the whole of it.

As the people turn their attention to the video, you will have time to catch a breath. Trying to keep a conversation going can be draining, you know. The conversation will then resume on a new angle. People will now be giving their views on what they just watched. Others could take the queue and also share the content they have on their gadgets. You all can then have something in common to speak about.

Exit politely

Sometimes, even after your best effort, the conversation cannot seem to gain traction. You do not have to suffer endlessly. You can excuse yourself. Begin by summarizing what you guys last spoke about. For instance, on the video above, you can say something like, 'that is a whole lot of money to expect a third-world country to pay back in such a short time.' Then ask to leave. Thank them for their time and state that you need to leave to attend to a different matter and walk out gracefully.

Chapter 22: Communicating with Difficult People

Difficult people thrive in defying logic; or do they have a different kind of logic? It's hard to tell. While some of them are oblivious of the negative impact of their attitude, others are fully aware of the distress they cause, and it does not bother them much.

Whenever you encounter an unreasonable person, the first instinct tells you to reciprocate the exact same attitude. And why not? They started it anyway, right? This is common in a business where disgruntled customers want to give everyone a piece of their mind. Sometimes they have a legitimate concern. Sometimes not. In fact, they could be on the wrong. Perhaps you should show them that you can yell too, right?

This sounds like an easy approach. However, if you're here reading this book on communications skills, you must be interested in improving your conversation intelligence. You're keen on developing your social skills, improving empathy, learning the art of persuasion and achieving successful relationships all around. Therefore, when you encounter difficult people, you must choose to be the bigger person and deal with the situation rationally.

Don't make demands

Once a person begins being unruly, it is tempting to also shout him into submission by ordering him to keep quiet, sit down, calm down, leave and so on. But remember you're dealing with a person who is already agitated. Additional orders will only make matters worse.

Involve others

If you're certain that you're in the right, involve other people. If you're at work, call your coworkers. If not, you can involve your family, friends, and even strangers. Maybe somebody else will bring a different approach and the person will listen.

Remain calm

The problem here is not feeling angry, but letting the anger control your actions. You can control your anger (we have covered that extensively in another topic) and remain calm. Surprise the aggressor who expects you to be equally angry. He'll realize that he's the only angry one. Now that sort of embarrassing; right? He's likely to calm down on his own volition. Remaining calm also gives you the clarity of thought that you need to evaluate the situation.

Disengage

If the person totally refuses to listen, you have the right to disengage and walk away from the negativity. Say something like 'I'll talk to you later when you calm down.' If you're in your premises, have security escort him out.

Avoid violence

In worst case scenario, the person might try to hit or push you. Get away before you're provoked to fight back. You might have come across that video of a McDonald's employee who was pushed by an aggressive customer, and she then turned and attacked him viciously. She had to be restrained by her colleagues. Interestingly, the court found the customer guilty of starting the aggression. She only acted in self-defense, albeit very fiercely. This is what a moment of provocation can do to you. This can happen even to the calmest among us. Walk away quickly before your senses lead you to fight back. You can involve the police if the case meets the threshold.

Evaluate the situation

For every difficult person that you deal with without losing your calm, give yourself a pat in the back. A lesson well-learned and practiced; right? As long as you remain grounded, you emerge as the bigger person. Remember the aggressor will also be evaluating the incident later. They'll most likely feel embarrassed that they were causing all the trouble while you managed to keep calm.

Can difficult people change? Yes, they can. Yes, they should. If you're willing to help, try to seek them out when they're in a good mood. Speak to them about their attitude and actions. They might see some sense. Give them time to go and reflect, and hopefully, they will change with time.

Chapter 23: Use Laughter to Lighten the Conversation

Throwing in a joke or two or a bunch into a conversation makes it a lot lighter, dissipates tension and gets the listeners glued. Whether it's a corporate talk or a casual conversation, the funny fellow always gets the audience.

Some people are naturally funny, others not quite. If you fall into the second category, as most people do, you can learn to be funny. You're not trying to be a comedian; the goal here is to use humor strategically to make the conversation interesting.

Here are some guidelines in developing and using humor in your conversations.

Use it to diffuse tension

You can apply similar humor in different situations around you to melt the tension and bring the people back to a rational conversation.

This applies when you're not naturally funny and you

need to put in some work. First, determine what makes you laugh. When you read or watch shows, what is it that you find funny? Is it the puns, rants or exaggeration? It is easier to develop your humor around what you find funny. Secondly, what is it that you say that gets people laughing even when you didn't intend to be funny? Is it the puns? Try working on those and using them more regularly.

Give the message priority

Don't get too excited about cracking jokes that you forget about your core content. We're using laughter here to lighten the conversation, meaning the main focus is on the conversation. If you're giving a formal presentation where you need to first write down your ideas, you don't have to include the jokes in the first draft. Dedicate the first draft to the message that you want to deliver. You can then weave in the jokes in the second draft.

Sound Natural

The jokes should blend in seamlessly into the rest of the content. Practice beforehand if you have to. Forced jokes bring in awkward moments at best. Long after you've spoken it, your listener realizes that it was supposed to be a joke. But it wasn't funny. You'll attract a chuckle at best, from a listener or two trying to be courteous. Not good at all for your impression.

Don't introduce a joke either. Just throw it in there like you're not even trying. Don't laugh at your own jokes, and definitely, don't start laughing before you crack the joke. In fact, you should look like you don't even think it's funny.

Avoid ridiculing others

Avoid poking fun directly to your listeners. Something may sound like a joke to you, while someone else hears something completely different. Make fun of things and events, not the people you're talking to. Make fun of your common challenges. It gives people the feeling of 'we're in this together.'

Teasing students over their poor performance, or employees over the company's losing streak, it not motivating them. You're just killing their spirits.

Remember to crack just enough jokes, not too many. If you're slotting in a joke after every five sentences, perhaps you should consider comedy. As long as you're engaging in normal conversation, use them only periodically. If you have mastered the art of using jokes to relieve tension, you will be better at conflict management.

Chapter 24: Developing Communication Skills

Okay, so you may not have been born with the natural gift of gab the way some people were, but there's some good news waiting for you. Everyone – yes, EVERYONE – can learn how to be an effective communicator. Thankfully, communication skills are something that can easily be developed and practiced on so you can get better progressively.

Before we begin, here is something to take note of – effective communication involves both verbal and non-verbal language. It is not just about the way that you speak, but also the manner in which you carry yourself, that makes you an effective communication overall. If you want to be successful, you are going to need to hone your skills in both of these areas.

Emphasize on Your Skills

Becoming effective at anything you want to do requires you to practice, often. The same goes for learning to communicate effectively. If you want to be successful with communicating effectively and professionally, you need to put a strong emphasis on your communication skills. Since active conversation is already a given, we are going to look at more solutions beyond this basic setting.

Take Communication Classes

Communication classes are often lead by teachers, mentors, or coaches who are effectively using communication in their own lives. As a result, they can teach you how to communicate more effectively in your own life as well.

Using communication classes as a means to begin practicing your communication skills provides you with a wonderful opportunity to have active, hands-on guidance during your learning experience. This also gives you the ability to practice with other students who are learning alongside you. For some people, learning at the same time as others makes the process a lot easier. Knowing that you are not practicing on someone who may be judging your skills means that you can eliminate the pressure and truly get some effective practice in. Furthermore, people gather at these classes specifically for the purpose of learning to communicate. As well, because you are practicing directly alongside a teacher, mentor, or coach, you can be given advice based on your specific skillset. If they recognize that you are excelling in one area but may be struggling in another area, for example, they can point this out to you and provide you with information to assist you in improving your skills.

Read as Often as You Can

Reading is another wonderful way to improve your communication skills. When you read, you gain the opportunity to learn more about how other people communicate. Through this process, you can learn about many techniques and practices that are unique to various areas of communication. For example, through actively reading you can quickly pick up on what types of words are regularly used in professional writing, versus that which are used in more casual writing pieces. This will allow you to understand what type of language is typically deemed acceptable in various circumstances. It can also help broaden your vocabulary and assist you in learning how to integrate various words into unique sentence structures.

When it comes to using reading as a tool to assist you in practicing your communication, you want to read as many different forms of written material as you can. Look toward reading newspapers, magazines, fiction and non-fiction novels, blog posts, and more. The more you diversify the materials that you use for this practice, the more you are going to be exposed to a variety of communication styles.

Practice with Other Successful Communicators

Regularly engaging in conversation with people who communicate at the level you wish to communicate at allows you to actively pick up on their skills and grow your own. When you converse with people who are already communicating at the level you desire to, it becomes easier to see how the various skills are used in practice. It also encourages you to communicate in this way so that you feel more natural and fluent in the conversation you are sharing.

There are many instances where you can find people who are communicating at the level you desire to communicate at. For example, if you intend to communicate professionally, conversing with those who are already conversing on a professional level is a great place to start. You will begin to expand your vocabulary into that unique element, as well as learn how to effectively use those new vocabulary words in active conversation. The same goes for anywhere else. The more we spend time with people who communicate and behave in a way that we desire to, the easier it is for us to integrate those new methods of communication and behavior into our own systems.

Use Your Skills All the Time

Lastly, if you truly want to have success with learning to communicate at a more advanced and effective level, you should be practicing your skills all the time. Those who communicate effectively do not turn their communication skills "on" or "off" from conversation to conversation. This would ultimately result in them not being able to communicate as effectively overall. Instead, they communicate with their new communication skills all of the time. Through regular and consistent practice, it becomes significantly easier to assimilate these new skills into their practice.

You should be using your new conversation skills on a daily basis with anyone you speak with. Whether it is family, friends, cashiers, co-workers, bosses, or otherwise, communicate in the same way on a consistent basis. When you do this, you will gain plenty of opportunity to expand your practice and skills. This will result in you communicating more effectively consistently, and with ease. There will be no considering "how" to communicate between person to person, because you will do it the same way every time: effectively and professionally.

Keep Things Simple

When we attempt to integrate difficult skills into our communication strategies, it can create a world of distraction and chaos. Trying to recall difficult strategies and integrate them in active practice is challenging, especially when you are likely already communicating beyond your present level of experience. Keeping things simple is necessary if you want to communicate effectively with other people.

When you attempt to add too many complex strategies and skills in place at any given time, effectively communicating can be challenging. Not only will you struggle to recall the many different strategies you are attempting to integrate, but your audience will also struggle to understand what you are attempting to communicate. There is no need for communication to be a difficult, complex, or over-done process. In fact, the very opposite tends to work far better.

Think about it: if you are trying to learn to communicate more effectively and with greater professionalism, stumbling over your words and taking several moments between sentences to attempt to recall all of your unique strategies will be a struggle. You are likely going to struggle to integrate any communication skills because you are attempting to integrate too many to begin with. Furthermore, the majority of people do not communicate at a complex level. Attempting to communicate with your audience with an advanced level of complexity may result in them becoming confused and not thoroughly understanding what it is that you are attempting to say. Most people like things straight forward and to the point. Keeping it clean and simple like this ensures that they know exactly what they are being told and prevents miscommunications from happening. Attempting to interpret too many different, potentially conflicted pieces of communication can become stressful and will result in both you and your audience being out of sync.

Simplifying the process means that you choose the most direct route to get to your point. You keep your words clean, simple, and clear. You directly tell your audience what it is that you are trying to communicate, and you use the best vocabulary to communicate your point perfectly. In doing so, it becomes significantly easier for them to understand what it is that you are trying to express to them. It also prevents you from getting confused in the process of actually trying to express it to begin with. Ultimately, what happens is that the conversation remains clear and consistent, and everyone understands what the purpose of the conversation is.

Be Clear with Your Message

Expanding off of the practice of simplicity, it is important that you are always clear with your message. Before you attempt to articulate yourself to someone else, know exactly what it is that you want to say. Being clear with your message ensures that everything you say is accurate to what you are thinking and feeling. You are able to then express yourself effectively, efficiently, and with professionalism.

Self-Awareness

Understanding your message comes from having a level of self-awareness that allows you to truly comprehend what your message is. For many of us, poor communication skills start from within. When we are unclear about what it is that we are truly feeling or thinking, it becomes significantly harder for us to communicate these feelings and thoughts to other individuals. Learning how to truly decipher the meanings of our thoughts and feelings and how they translate into what we want to share with the other person is important.

When you are communicating with someone, before you share your message, take a moment to think about what it truly is. Often, the initial thoughts or feelings we have may not be clear or in alignment with what it is that we are actually attempting to convey to the other person. For example, in some situations we may be elated that someone has offered us something, but we are not actually wanting to receive the offer, we are simply grateful that it was made. Alternatively, we may hear something and initially become angry, only to later realize we were actually jealous or disappointed and not actually angry. These types of confusions within our own thoughts and feelings can result in us not communicating them effectively with others, because we are not communicating them effectively with ourselves. Taking your time and learning to decipher what it is that you are truly feeling and thinking is the first step in gaining clarity around your message. Once you are clear in what that is, it becomes significantly easier to share that with other people.

Know Your Perspective

In addition to knowing what you are feeling or thinking, you also need to know your perspective. The way that you can find out your perspective is to ask yourself "why" you are feeling or thinking the way that you are. Doing this will allow you to gain some clarity around the feelings and thoughts themselves. This will help you take them from just a thought or a feeling and turn them into an actual message. For example, "I'm angry" becomes, "I am disappointed that you would say something like that to me." This allows us to take the initial reaction or thought toward something and evolve it into a true perspective and message that we can share with the other person.

Knowing your perspective is also rooted in self-awareness. You must be self-aware enough to be able to dig deeper into the initial reactions you have so that you can translate them into a proper message. Taking your time and enforcing these self-awareness practices will ensure that you are clear on what your message is before you even attempt to share it with someone else. Being clear in yourself makes it significantly easier for you to clearly express yourself to someone else.

Express it Clearly

The key now is to take your time, choose the appropriate words, and communicate yourself in a way that clearly expresses where you are coming from, and why. Clearly sharing your message, the first time prevents you from having to repeatedly create supporting statements surrounding your message so that you can provide clarification on the various areas where you did not effectively express yourself.

Being able to clearly express your message assists in warding off unnecessary experiences that coincide with miscommunications. When we do not effectively express ourselves, we may inadvertently put someone in a position where they become defensive or upset by what we have said. We may also create confusion around our message and make it more challenging for our audience to fully understand us. Even if we end up creating clarity in the end, they will have become so confused by the beginning portion of our attempt that it will not be nearly as effective as it could have been had we expressed ourselves properly the first time. So, it is absolutely crucial that you develop clarity in your message before sharing it, and then that you share it directly and clearly.

Slow Yourself Down

Often, we find ourselves struggling to effectively communicate with others because we are attempting to communicate too quickly. All too often, we communicate by immediately and automatically expressing the first thing that comes to our minds. This is not something that we are taught, but rather it is something that we learn and continue doing because we are not taught a more effective method of communication. This very practice is responsible for us frequently saying the wrong things, expressing ourselves in a way that does not accurately reflect our thoughts, opinions or feelings, or otherwise communicating in a way that lacks clarity and efficiency. When we stop communicating automatically and begin intentionally thinking about how we wish to communicate, it becomes easier for us to express ourselves accurately to what we are actually feeling and thinking.

Give Yourself a Moment to Think

Whenever you are communicating with anyone, always give yourself a moment to think before responding to the other person. Taking this moment each time we are communicating, especially with important or sensitive topics, enables us to be absolutely certain that we are going to communicate in a way that is appropriate to how we are actually thinking and feeling.

Often, people automatically respond by immediately saying what comes to mind. These thoughts are typically unfiltered and rarely express exactly what we mean. As a result, we end up finding ourselves entering situations where we begin reconsidering the conversation later and wishing we had expressed ourselves differently. This happens because we did not take the time to accurately consider what it was that we wanted to express the first time around. When we slow down mid-conversation and use this as an opportunity to become clear and direct in our communication, the entire nature of the conversation changes. We express ourselves honestly and openly, but with tact and consideration for the others involved in the conversation. As a result, we end up finding ourselves "regretting" our expression significantly less later on because we did so effectively in the first place. Rather than wishing we had done so differently, we know that we can honestly stand behind what we said because it accurately reflected what we wanted to say.

Do Not Feel Pressured to Respond Before You Know

Although you do not want to keep the person you are conversing with waiting for an incredibly long period of time, it is important that you do not feel pressured to respond before you actually know what it is that you want to say.

The less pressure you apply to yourself to answer right away, or to take a specific amount of time before answering, the easier it will be for you to take a moment to tune in with yourself and choose an accurate answer. This may take a second, or it may take several seconds. Rarely will it last upward of about 30 seconds. That is, unless you put too much pressure on yourself. Feeling pressured to answer right away, or to wait a set amount of time before answering, makes it difficult for you to accurately tune in to what you are thinking and discover a way to communicate it. Instead, you want to eliminate the pressure. You are not required to respond immediately, nor are you required to respond after any preset amount of time. Instead, you should respond once you know what the honest thought is that you are thinking and wanting to express.

Ensure You Are Understood

Many times, miscommunication happens because we are not clearly understood by the person we are communicating with. As clearly as we may feel we have expressed ourselves, the way it is coming across to the other person may not be clear enough for them to truly comprehend what we meant versus what we said.

Ensuring that you have been understood by the person you are communicating with takes some skill, a few easy steps, and a willingness to understand that you may have contributed to the miscommunication if one does occur.

Look for Clues of Understanding

If a person understood you, there are many signs that they may express. Nodding their head in agreement, having an open and soft body language that is receptive, and looking clearly at you are all good physical clues that the person you are talking to understands what you have said. Furthermore, they should be able to easily relay back to you what it is that you have shared with them. While not every conversation will include the other person repeating back what you said to them, the following responses they provide should clearly align with what you have shared. If they communicate back with you in a way that is very clear to what you have already shared with them and expresses no clear signs of confusion or misunderstanding, there is a good chance that what they have heard and understood is in alignment with what you have said. Other ways to ensure that the person understood what you meant may arise if you have asked a person to do something and they fulfill the duty properly based on the information you have provided them with. If the duty is fulfilled improperly, there is a good chance that the communication between you and them was not clearly articulated.

If someone does not understand what you have said to them, their clues will be completely different. Their heads may be completely still with their eyebrows pinched and a somewhat confused look on their face, expressing that they are not entirely clear on what it is that you are trying to communicate to them. They may cross their arms or grasp at one arm with their opposing hand to show that they are feeling confused and potentially nervous in the conversation. They may also tune out eventually if they feel that they truly are not getting it and that the level of communication is not improving despite them attempting to gain clarity. Verbal cues that they are not fully understanding what you have said include asking several questions to clarify what you meant, as well as providing answers that are not clearly in alignment with what it is that you meant. If the conversation warrants them repeating your message back to you, they will not be able to do so clearly because they will not be sure as to what the message actually was.

It is important that you look for these cues on the person that you are talking to.

Consider How You Have Contributed to Misunderstandings

When misunderstandings do arise, which they do from time to time no matter how well we attempt to communicate with others, it is important that we look at the situation objectively. Often, we want to quickly jump into a defensive mode and point our fingers at the other person, blaming them for the misunderstanding. It feels easier to blame them for not "getting it" than it is to blame ourselves for the fact that we may have not communicated ourselves clearly enough. Although this may make ourselves feel better in regard to who is to blame, it will not assist us in accurately and effectively clearing up the byproducts of the miscommunication itself.

First off, when we point blame at someone else it results in them also entering a defensive state of mind. This means that the miscommunication will further fester and become a complete argument or conflict between yourself and another individual. Once this occurs, the likelihood that effective and positive communication skills will be applied to this conversation drops significantly. Arguments, defensiveness, and conflict often lead to us communicating poorly as we automatically say what comes to mind as an attempt to deflect the conflict and protect ourselves from feeling hurt or attacked by the other person. When two people enter this state, the conflict becomes harder to resolve, sometimes requiring mediation for positive and effective communication to begin to be used once more.

Second, blaming the other person does not allow us to clearly identify where the communication went wrong to begin with. This is because we have quickly resorted to an argument of trying to identify who is right and who is wrong, rather than an opportunity for effective communication to ensue. As a result, we are not able to learn from the experience and therefore it becomes more likely to happen again at some point in the future.

The reality is, in these scenarios, most often it is both people who are to blame. One person failed to communicate effectively in the first place, and the second person then failed to communicate that they were not completely clear on what was being told to them to begin with. As a result, both have contributed to unclear communication practices, and both have failed to mention that they were unclear to begin with. Then, both parties take their lack of clarity with them and find themselves feeling confused and uncertain about what was gained from the conversation. They may also end up taking hurt and guilt with them from anything that may have come up during the conflict that was shared.

Use This as an Opportunity to Grow Stronger in Your Skills

Even if you are entirely to blame for the conversation resulting in miscommunication and confusion, ask for assistance in understanding why. Even if you felt you communicated clearly and it was the other person who did not explain that they were unclear with what you had said, ask for assistance in understanding why. As well, attempt to recall the conversation in your mind and see if you can pick up any clues that you may have missed in the moment that proved that the other person was not completely certain as to what was being communicated to them.

Once you have done this, you can then take the chance to identify how the conversation could have been handled differently. You can look for new opportunities to search for understanding from the person you are conversing with in the future, as well as develop new skills to avoid any mistakes you may have made that resulted in the confusion or lack of understanding. This will ensure that you grow from the unfortunate situation, rather than it becoming even more frustrating and potentially leading to further miscommunications of the same degree in the future.

Consider Your Body Language

As you already likely know, your body language plays a major role in how you communicate with other people. Your body language will either support your message, contradict it, or share an entirely different message altogether. If you want to effectively communicate with other people, you need to learn how you can properly consider your body language to ensure that you are communicating properly with the person you are talking to.

Our body language has the potential to contradict us in many ways, and for many reasons. As a result, we may end up inadvertently sending the wrong messages to people during our conversations. Let's explore some examples whereby your body language may result in you not effectively expressing yourself and your message to the person you are communicating with, and why these situations may happen.

Use Appropriate Styles of Communication

When you are communicating, it is necessary that you use appropriate styles of communication to ensure that you are being properly received by your audience. Using appropriate styles of communication will ensure that you are able to effectively share what you are thinking and feeling without miscommunications taking place. It also means that you will be able to communicate in a way that your audience can easily receive. You do not want to be communicating in the wrong style and tone for your audience, or you may disrupt your effective communication patterns and find yourself being overtaken by misunderstandings.

Learning to communicate appropriately requires you to identify your audience, communicate in alignment with them, use appropriate vocabulary, and stay on the side of caution whenever necessary. If you implement these strategies, then you will be able to easily communicate in accordance with the audience you are talking to.

Conclusion

Thanks for making it through to the end of this book! Effective communication doesn't have to be very difficult. It only needs the right strategies and determination to master communication.

You are now armed with the knowledge and the skills that you need to become a more effective communicator. The next step is to apply the techniques that you have learned in this book and start practicing them in your everyday life and in your workplace to begin communicating more effectively and impress others with your newfound mastery of this underrated skill.

Take your new knowledge and start applying it to your life. You can certainly see that with effective communication skills, it is much easier to find happiness and success in life.

These skills take time and practice, so be sure to go easy on yourself and allow yourself the opportunity to implement them in a way that will be effective for you. It will likely result in your message becoming confusing, and your audience not truly understanding what it is that you are trying to say. Even if you do manage to finally get it across, they will likely already be too confused from everything you mentioned beforehand to actually get what you mean.

Keep this book close while working on your communication. It includes all of the information that you need to be successful. This means that it will serve as a reference now and in the future when you want to sharpen your more advanced communication skills.

About the Author

Diego is a young entrepreneur who started his career in the real estate market about 20 years ago. Today, after attending and completing the Master in Coaching and with the title of Advanced Master Practitioner in Neuro-Linguistic Programming, he works with entrepreneurs and sportsmen to bring them to personal success. Use effective communication as a tool for achieving your goals and your clients' goals